Ignorant Yobs?: Low Attainers in a Global Knowledge Economy

What happens to young people who are defined as lower attainers or having learning difficulties in a global knowledge economy?

How do we stop those with learning difficulties or disabilities being seen as social problems or simply as consumers of resources?

Governments in developed countries are driven by the belief that in a global economy all citizens should be economically productive, yet they are still not clear about the relationship between the education of low attainers and the labour market. *Ignorant Yobs?: Low Attainers in a Global Knowledge Economy* examines this international phenomenon, exploring how those with learning difficulties are treated in a world economy where even low-skilled jobs require qualifications.

This unique book provides an examination of countries which converge on the issue of the low attaining population, despite differing on political, economic and cultural dimensions. In doing so, it considers some thorny issues at the forefront of education policy and provision:

- the increasing competitive stratification within education systems;
- the impact of governments who have put competition in the labour market at the heart of their policies;
- social control of potentially disruptive groups, social cohesion and the human rights agenda;
- the expansion of a special education industry driven by the needs of middle class, aspirant and knowledgeable parents, anxious about the success of their 'less able' children.

Written by an internationally renowned scholar, *Ignorant Yobs?: Low Attainers in a Global Knowledge Economy* synthesises a range of complex, highly topical issues and suggests how those with learning difficulties might, with government and employer support, contribute to a flexible labour market. This book, using original discussions in England, the USA, Germany, Malta and Finland, will be of interest to a wide audience of policy-makers, practitioners, administrators, and politicians, in addition to undergraduate, postgraduate and research students and academics.

Sally Tomlinson is Emeritus Professor at Goldsmiths College, London University and Senior Research Fellow in the Department of Education, University of Oxford, UK.

Ignorant Yobs?: Low Attainers in a Global Knowledge Economy

Sally Tomlinson

 Routledge
Taylor & Francis Group

LONDON AND NEW YORK

First published 2013
by Routledge
2 Park Square, Milton Park, Abingdon, Oxon OX14 4RN

Simultaneously published in the USA and Canada
by Routledge
711 Third Avenue, New York, NY 10017

Routledge is an imprint of the Taylor & Francis Group, an informa business

© 2013 Sally Tomlinson

British Library Cataloguing in Publication Data
A catalogue record for this book is available from the British Library

Library of Congress Cataloging in Publication Data
Tomlinson, Sally.
  Ignorant yobs? : low attainers in a global knowledge economy /
  Authored by Sally Tomlinson.
     p. cm.
  Includes index.
  ISBN 978-0-415-52576-3 (hbk) — ISBN 978-0-415-52577-0 (pbk)
  — ISBN 978-0-203-11974-7 (ebk) 1. Learning disabled—
  Vocational guidance.   2. People with disabilities—Vocational
  guidance.   3. Special education—Cross-cultural studies.
  4. Learning disabled—Education.   5. Labor market.   I. Title.
  HV1568.5.T66 2013
  362.3'84—dc23   2012025047

ISBN: 978-0-415-52576-3 (hbk)
ISBN: 978-0-415-52577-0 (pbk)
ISBN: 978-0-203-11974-7 (ebk)

Typeset in Galliard
by RefineCatch Limited, Bungay, Suffolk

Cover image: *The Guardian*, published on 17 April 2012; illustrator:
Kipper Williams; caption: Finance cartoon.

MIX
Paper from
responsible sources
FSC
www.fsc.org   FSC® C004839

Printed and bound in Great Britain by the MPG Books Group

For John Rex 1926–2011
A scholar with integrity and the courage of his convictions

Contents

Acknowledgements

With grateful thanks to the Leverhulme Trust whose grant enabled me to carry out the research for this book.

Special thanks to all the participants: principals, head teachers, teachers and administrators, who made time to talk to me and to the students who allowed me to observe them.

Thanks also to colleagues from five countries for help and discussion: Liz Atkins, Margaret S. Archer, George A. Borg, David Connor, Mary Darmanin, Hubert Ertl, Peter Flaschel, Vicki Graf, Geoff Hayward, Jarkko Hautamäki, Hugo Kremer, Reeta Mietola, Michael O'Brien, Lela Rondeau, Sigrid Luchtenberg, Alison Wolf, and to my readers Hugh Lauder and John Richardson.

List of abbreviations

ADHD	Attention deficit hyperactivity disorder
ASD	Autistic spectrum disorder
ASDAN	Award Scheme Development and Accreditation Network
BESD	Behavioural, emotional and social difficulty
BTEC	Business and Technology Education Council
CAF	Common Assessment Framework
CSE	Certificate of Secondary Education
DES	Department for Education and Science
DfCSF	Department for Children, Schools and Families
DfE	Department for Education
DfEE	Department for Education and Employment
DfES	Department for Education and Skills
DTI	Department for Trade and Industry
E2E	Entry to Employment
EAL	English as an Additional Language
EBD	Emotionally and behaviourally disturbed
EET	Education, Employment or Training
EFA	Education Funding Agency
EHCP	Education, Health and Care Plan
EMA	Education Maintenance Allowance
EMR	Educably mentally retarded
ESN	Educationally subnormal
ESN-M	Educationally subnormal (moderate)
ESRC	Economic and Social Research Council
FE	Further Education College
FSM	Free School Meals
GCSE	General Certificate of Secondary Education
GNVQ	General National Vocational Qualification
IEP	Individual Education Programme
ILO	International Labour Office
IPE	Individualised Plan for Employment
IPPR	Institute for Public Policy Research

LD	Learning Disability
LDD	Learning Difficulty or Disability
LSA	Learning Support Assistant
LSC	Learning and Skills Council
MALD	Moderate and additional Learning Difficulty
MCAST	Malta College of Arts, Science and Technology
MLD	Moderate learning difficulty
MoVE	Modelling of Vocational Excellence
MSC	Manpower Services Commission
MSEC	Malta Secondary Education Certificate
NED	Non-educated Delinquent
NEET	Not in Education, Employment or Training
NVQ	National Vocational Qualification
NCVQ	National Council for Vocational Qualifications
OCD	Oppositional conduct disorder
OCR	Oxford, Cambridge, Royal Society of Arts Examinations
ODD	Oppositional defiance disorder
OECD	Organisation for Economic Co-operation and Development
Ofsted	Office for Standards in Education
PISA	Programme for International Student Assessment
PMLD	Profound and multiple learning difficulty
PRU	Pupil Referral Unit
QCF	Qualifications and Curriculum Framework
RCCCFM	*Report of the Royal Commission on the Care and Control of the Feeble-minded*
RSA	Royal Society of Arts
SEN	Special Educational Needs
SENCO	Special Educational Needs Co-ordinator
SKOPE	Centre for Skills, Knowledge and Organisational Performance
SLD	Severe learning difficulty
SPLD	Specific learning difficulty
SWG	Student Welfare Group
TEC	Training and Enterprise Council
TVEI	Technical and Vocational Educational Initiative
UTC	University Technical Colleges
VET	Vocational education and training
YOPS	Youth Opportunities Programme
YPLA	Young People's Learning Agency
YTS	Youth Training Scheme

Introduction

The hooligan, defective, feeble-minded and delinquent loafers of 1910 have become the yobs, chavs, NEETS and scroungers of 2010.[1]

This book is about the expanding numbers of young people in developed countries who are variously regarded as lower attainers, have learning difficulties and/or special educational needs, and what is happening to them. The past 30 years have seen a widespread acceptance of beliefs that all citizens in nation-states are subject to the forces of globalisation and global economic markets. All national governments now believe that higher levels of educational attainment and skills training are necessary for successful competition in knowledge-driven economies. All young people are urged to invest in their own human capital and constantly learn new skills, competing with each other in stratified education systems and uncertain job markets. In this scenario knowledge becomes a marketable commodity and those demonstrating high levels are prized above manual, craft and physically-skilled workers. The old divisions of those deemed suitable for academic or vocational life courses take on new meanings.

While education systems in developed countries were expanding during the later-nineteenth and early-twentieth century, from the mid-twentieth century there was a rapid expansion as groups previously excluded or given only a minimal education were drawn into lengthened formal systems, usually at lower levels of schooling. This was particularly true of those who were regarded as having difficulties in learning to minimal levels of numeracy and literacy, being low attainers in formal testing, failing to achieve to constantly raised qualification levels or acquiring one or more of a variety of expanding descriptions eventually bundled from the 1980s into a shorthand of special educational needs. Characteristics of those drawn into expanding systems at lower levels were that they were predominantly from lower social classes, with more males than females and with an over-representation of racial and ethnic minorities. Rationalisation for this educational expansion for all groups has centred round the political, commercial and social interests that all young people should be economically productive, and not reliant on unemployment or other welfare benefits. While policy, practice and literature on the provision and expansion of vocational education and training and special education has largely remained separate, here they are brought together. Educational expansion has included an expansion of education for the working classes, and worldwide moves towards inclusive education have meant that mainstream schools and colleges now incorporate a range of students regarded as having learning difficulties and disabilities. They are all now expected to participate post-14 or 16 in some kind of education and training for a potential working future, or failing that, be prepared for independent living. In addition there has been an expansion of middle-class demands for recognition and resources for their children who have difficulty in learning in competitive school environments, which has helped fuel an expanding and expensive 'SEN industry' (Tomlinson 2012a). Parents are driven by anxieties that in competitive education and training systems their less-able children will not find or keep work, although middle-class parents are still likely to avoid placement of their young on lower-level vocational courses. The expansion of education systems has led to an expansion of institutional arrangements, resources and funding for all these lower attaining young people, and the whole edifice of mass education in a global economy is now underpinned by expanded provision for lower achievers and those with learning difficulties or disengagement.

A further justification for the expansion of education for these young people centres round the social control of groups who are likely to be potentially disruptive to the running of the society, and more provision for disengaged, disaffected and disruptive young people is a necessary political tool as well as an economic project. While ideologies of benevolent and paternalistic humanitarianism (Richardson and Powell 2011, Tomlinson 2012b) still provide a moral framework in which many professionals work, particularly with an increase in numbers of therapeutic professionals, by the early twenty-first century attitudes towards potentially workless lower attainers had become more punitive and reminiscent of early twentieth-century views. The hooligan, dull, delinquent slum-monkeys (Humphries 1981) who so agitated the late Victorian and Edwardian upper and middle classes in England, have become the louts, yobs, chavs, scum, and workshy scroungers who in the twenty-first century continue to disturb more fortunate citizens (Connelly 2011, Jones 2011). It is worth stressing at the outset, that the recognition, classification and provision for young people who do not achieve well in education or the job market is a social categorisation of economically and socially weaker groups, who can be treated unequally, differently and often punitively by those with power.

The book is intended to provide some information and discussion around the following:

- What is happening to young people in developed countries who post-14 are regarded as lower achievers, having learning difficulties or special needs, and how are they currently defined?

- How have education systems expanded to take account of these young people, and what sort of education and training programmes are in place for them?
- What is the relationship between the development of an expanded global economy and a 'knowledge economy', and what is the place of lower attainers in this economy?

Thirty years ago it was possible to suggest that as modern industrial societies increasingly demanded qualifications and credentials acquired through mainstream schooling, to be categorised out of this into special or segregated provision represented the ultimate in non-achievement (Tomlinson 2012b). Now non-achievement, unless there are absolutely compelling reasons, cannot be tolerated in knowledge economies. Because the dominant ideology is that education plays a major role in economic competitiveness, all individuals, whatever their learning capacities, must develop their own human capital and conform to accepted standards of economic and social behaviour. The UK government was certainly concerned that young people identified as having special educational needs should not be low attainers, and in 2010 published a paper on *Breaking the link between special educational needs and low attainment* (DfCSF. 2010). Numbers in the groups in question – lower attainers, those with learning difficulties, disabilities and disaffection – vary historically and comparatively, and between schools, regions and countries. In England, the initial focus of the book, the 'bottom 40 per cent' of attainers continue to cause anxiety, especially the 1.7 million children classed as having special educational needs, and the overlapping group of over one million post-16 not in education, employment or training In the USA, the future of the learning disabled and those who drop out or do not obtain a high school diploma is problematic, as for those in Germany who leave the Hauptschule or a special school without a certificate. In Malta, 40 per cent of young people leave education and training altogether at 16, and in Finland, there are still students in need of special support after 16. In all developed countries it is the lower attainers and the 'special' who make up the majority of students on lower-level vocational courses in schools and colleges, and they are more likely to be from lower social classes and minority groups.

The book is based on a study of the policies, practices and views of a selection of personnel who make educational and vocational arrangements for lower attainers post-14, in mainstream and special schools and colleges. An initial overview of the literature on learning difficulties, low achievement, special and vocational education was undertaken, as was a review of some literature on globalisation and the links between education and work in national and global economies. The enormous amount of research, academic and practitioner writing, government legislation, guidance and statistical information in all these areas meant that it was only possible to be selective of the literature. Information on current (2010–11) policies and practices was sought by visiting schools, colleges and administrators in three English local authorities, and also some discussion was held with academics and practitioners knowledgeable about vocational education and lower attainers.[2] To provide some comparative information on similarities and differences in what was offered post-14 to those deemed to be lower achievers or 'special' students in other countries, visits were made to schools and colleges in the USA (New York and Los Angeles), Germany (North Rhine Westphalia), Malta and Finland. Some 77 discussions were held and there was some limited observation of students on vocational courses. Information from overseas discussions was not intended to provide rigorous case studies but to consider differences as well as similarities between what is now a highly centralised English system, a smaller centralised system (Malta), two areas largely decentralised by virtue of federal state organisation (USA and Germany) and a small decentralised system (Finland).

Some theoretical considerations

Although the following chapters are empirical and descriptive, all the policies and practices are dependent on some implicit social and economic theory held by the policy makers and participants. The interpretations made about what is happening and in whose interests needs to be made clear.[3] Here there is an attempt to understand current political economy – the study of the production, distribution and consumption of wealth and how this affects young people, and to understand the expansion of education systems in modern capitalist nation-states and the links to changing notions of social class and status in these nation-states. Education systems, their expansion, changes and what is offered to young people often appears to be in a permanently dynamic state. But education systems do not develop spontaneously, they do not mysteriously adapt to social requirements and they do not necessarily develop in order to benefit groups of young people. The systems develop their characteristics because of the goals pursued by people who control them and have vested interests in their development in particular ways (Archer 1979). Changes in the amount, form, organisation and provision of expanded education and training for young people happens because those with power can impose their views and goals on others. In doing so, the powerful are usually driven by some kind of ideological belief. In education, political groups usually claim to be maintaining or changing the system by appeals to tradition, usually traditions which are directed to maintaining a given social order, or on the benefits which some groups can obtain from change. Thus the traditional virtue of individual contribution to wealth creation via the regular participation of all young people in the economy is part of current political ideology in many countries, even though the system will not prepare them all properly to participate, and they will not share equally in the wealth produced. Ideological beliefs in the assumed tendency of less-educated working class young people, if not suitably controlled, to participate in antisocial and criminal behaviour, has traditionally provided a rationale for punitive and policing sanctions for some young people.

Governments in modern capitalist nation-states[4] are overseeing and encouraging a vast expansion of education and training, for reasons which those in control of policy and practice are not always clear about. Groups who were previously excluded or received minimal schooling are now included in formal schooling for longer and longer periods. Groups who previously monopolised privileged kinds of education leading to guaranteed employment now face threats of status and employment competition with larger numbers who aspire or are coerced into more formal schooling and its assessments. In order to retain privileges, elite groups support the reconstitution of segregative policies and provisions. Whether operating through centralised or decentralised control, governments face the ill-understood demands of a global economy and its effects on national economies. They face the management of new kinds of knowledge and technology, the expectations and assertive strategies of competing interest groups – notably private business and employers, professional educators and ancillary professions, faith groups, parents and students, and also the perceived need to certify, accredit or otherwise provide rationales for the expanding numbers of courses and programmes. They also must accommodate human rights and social justice claims that all young people should be included in expanding education systems, and there is a rhetoric that education can promote social cohesion.

From the 1980s changes within capitalist states and the rise of competitive market ideologies placed educational changes and reforms firmly within economic imperatives. Post-welfare societies (Tomlinson 2005) rapidly became market states, with public institutions encouraged or required to deregulate, privatise and contract out services. Much of education in England has been reconstructed into a series of private businesses, and current educational expansion is predicated on political claims that economic development and competition in a global economy requires more and higher levels of education, and labour markets require flexible, enterprising workers for a knowledge-based economy (Jessop 2002: 168). Political claims are made that education is a necessary route to employment and social mobility and thus all groups need more of it to higher levels, although in the economic climate of the twenty-first century, some hypocrisy was necessary to explain away the increase in nepotism and family influence in obtaining higher-level employment. Evidence concerning the reality of claims made is often counter-intuitive. Wolf pointed out (2002: xi) that politicians' faith in education has been fuelled by a set of clichés about the nature of the twenty-first century world, some of which are demonstrably untrue. The notion of knowledge economies is contested, the link between spending on education and economic growth is problematic, and education even to high levels is no longer a guarantee of secure employment. Brown and his colleagues have graphically explored the breaking of the 'opportunity bargain' in some Western countries, whereby the middle classes felt assured that investing in education would secure for their children a continuing comfortable life and prosperity. It is no longer the case that greater investment in education will automatically lead to rewarding jobs (Brown, Lauder and Ashton 2011). In addition, the ways different kinds of education are distributed does not lead to social cohesion, and those educated to high levels may invest their knowledge in the pursuit of individual greed and activities detrimental to the society as a whole (as the activities of some bankers and financiers in the first decade of the twenty-first century in the USA and UK might illustrate). Those who have invested in their own human capital at lower levels through courses, time and money, may not find employment, but face punitive sanctions if they do not work. Governments have always found it easier to blame individuals for their failure to find work rather than invest in job creation.

Expanded education

Theoretical interest in why education systems expand, how educational institutions emerge and are elaborated with proliferating provision and why systems develop differently in different countries, has not been overwhelming (but see Archer 1979, 1988, 2008, Green 1990, Fuller and Rubinson 1992, Green, Preston and Janmaat 2006, Richardson and Powell 2011, Wolf 2002). Public education systems, as Green noted, should be understood in relation to the historical development of new nation-states. Education in emerging states embodied 'a new universalism that acknowledged that education was applicable to all groups in society and could serve a variety of social needs', although serving the interests of the dominant classes in a society, who often reserved the privileges of private non-state education for themselves (Green 1990: 79). While some groups, religious orders for example, could claim humanitarian interest in the education of the 'lower orders', it remains the case that education systems develop and change out of struggles between competing interest groups. Beneficiaries of existing kinds of schooling may resist change, as for example the English 'public' schools and their powerful associations continue to do, or assertive groups may substitute their own schools, as newer faith groups are doing. If assertive groups gain the support of political and business elites new types of school can emerge. In England for example, the post-1988 city technology colleges, the post-2000 academies, the post-2009 emergence of free schools and university technology colleges, in the USA the charter school movement, all illustrate assertive business, political and parental influence.

State education systems, comprising nationwide collections of institutions and personnel devoted to formal education are, in developed countries, enormous in size and complexity and enormously expensive. Education, in terms of providers, resources and numbers participating, is part of a large global industry and what is regarded as valuable knowledge is a commodity which can be bought and sold via state and private agencies. Education is political in the widest sense, and the forms that education systems take at any time is the result of the competing interests and ideologies noted above, with winners and losers in the competition being a necessary complement. Those in powerful positions can determine the amount and kind of education offered to various groups, with superior groups traditionally using a 'strategic maintenance of ignorance' (Archer 1988: 190) to limit the amounts and kind of education and educational resources offered to subordinate groups. In most of Europe, as Judt (2005: 391) pointed out, up to the 1950s most children left school at 12 or 14 – the grammar schools, lycees and gymnasiums of Europe, with their classical curricula, being 'the preserve of a ruling elite'. In England political elites had done their best, during the later nineteenth and early twentieth centuries, to limit the education offered to the mass of the population, and also to denigrate education which did not conform to the public school academic curriculum. An illustration of this was the wide variety of higher grade schools in England which by the 1890s were teaching science and technical subjects, but which the then Board of Education, staffed by men from public schools and Oxbridge, and with a permanent secretary 'who had a particular loathing for vocational and technical education' (Vlaeminke 1990: 67), managed to downgrade and impose a favoured model of humanities-based schooling. One consequence of this is that over a hundred years later there is still a downgrading of vocational and technical education in favour of academic subjects, the ability to parse a Latin sentence being held in higher esteem than the knowledge of how to mend a low-carbon boiler. In addition attempts to use education to create more cohesive societies usually founder on the contradiction that mass educational developments were never oriented towards a common good, but developed from sectional social, political and religious interests, often in competition with each other, which has the effect of dividing groups, notably by social class and ethnicity, rather than creating cohesion.

Once a particular form of education takes hold it influences future educational change and governments have great influence in determining the goals, size and funding of the system. In centralised systems governments assume they can both macro- and micro-manage on a national scale, although in decentralised systems there can be more negotiations between regions, local states or local authorities. Interest groups external to education can increasingly influence educational aims and expansion. Business leaders and employers have been recorded, from the nineteenth century onwards, as complaining about the poor quality products of education, and high-level business leaders, politicians and economists, in their annual soirée at Davos in Switzerland, regularly complain about the failure of education systems to prepare young people for economic conditions and the slow pace of educational change (Gates 2010). External pressure from international comparative testing, notably through the OECD's programme for international student assessment (PISA) leaves governments increasingly agitated about their country's place in international league tables. In efforts to improve educational levels, governments have brought in more private and business providers. Despite the wealth of developed countries with public education systems, there is private provision at all levels, preschool, special schools, vocational and trade schools, business schools, faith schools and universities, with private and for-profit groups being encouraged to take over, or supplement public provision.

Groups internal to education, professional educators and teachers at all levels, administrators, ancillary professionals, academics from various disciplines and others have influence over public education, although central government control over funding and resources makes it difficult for some groups to have political leverage. Teachers unions vary in the influence they have. In England the National Union of Teachers is largely ignored by government, although head teacher associations, notably the Independent [private] Heads Associations have some influence. In Germany, the Special School Teachers Union has been extremely influential in resisting moves towards more inclusive schooling. In the USA and the UK, medical and pharmaceutical interests in special education have expanded, with over a million children in the USA reportedly prescribed drugs for behavioural conditions, notably the drug Ritalin, which made its patenting company US$464 million in 2010. Parents and other pressure groups have, over the years, become more influential in seeking to influence the classification and placement of their children. In promising more parental choice in education, governments have found their policies rebounding as more parents began to exercise their 'rights'. In the USA parents have historically used litigation and the force of law to challenge decisions on their children's schooling. In Britain the use of litigation was slower to take off, but is now increasingly used, especially in the area of special education. Law firms now advertise their services and benefit from giving advice and litigation. Governments can ignore parental criticism of schooling, mobilise parental support for their favoured kinds of school, seek to placate them by notionally offering more choice of school, or turn them into vigilantes, policing schools and criticising teachers. Competition between schools, which in England are now largely run as individual businesses, and competition between students for enhanced test results, encourages parental dissatisfaction and criticism. In England current government policy that the GCSE examinations should favour traditional academic rather than vocational subjects, encourages schools, parents and labour markets, to regard vocational qualifications as of lower value. It is still the case that education ministers and their civil servants are largely products of the private school system,[5] and, despite using a rhetoric that education should cater for the needs of employers and the economy, have little understanding of vocational education. It is not far removed from the situation noted of the Board of Education in 1900, that 'education is administered by people entirely without first-hand acquaintance with the proletarian class of education they control. They lack imagination and they lack enthusiasm although many of them burst with brains' (Spencer 1938: 313).

Plan of the book

The first chapter briefly examines the realities of globalisation and the extent to which national governments can control their own economies and plan their education systems. The rhetoric of a global knowledge economy in which low skills are an enemy to growth, and high skills the key to competitiveness, is countered by the reality that developed countries still do require low-skill work, although paying low wages and increasingly now requiring some kind of qualification. Much of this work is done by lower attainers, although it is still an under-researched question as to how far lower attainers and those with disabilities are incorporated into developed economies. The chapter also notes the state of the English national economy and its unemployment problems.

The next three chapters concentrate on what is happening to low attainers and the 'special' in England. Chapter 2 notes that who gets defined as a lower attainer, having special needs or a disability, depends on current definitions of attainment and normality, which varies at different historical times, in different countries, in different schools and between different professions. It offers examples of historical and current confusion as to how to define lower attainers – from the feeble-minded and dull to the dyslexic and disruptive. England is an example of a system which has become heavily centralised, with a diversity of competitive educational institutions, and this diversity has encouraged more separation by social class and ethnicity. Lower attainers are predominantly the children of working- or non-working class parents, with high representation of some minority groups, refugees and second-language speakers. The chapter explores the simultaneous expansion of special education services and personnel, with the increasing inclusion in mainstream education of more young people with disabilities and learning difficulties. It also notes the needs of middle class and aspirant parents who claim classification and funding for those of their children who are unlikely to achieve well in competitive market-driven school systems. Chapter 3 addresses the issue that at post-14 and 16 young people, whether classed as having special educational needs or being lower attainers, are now encouraged or coerced into considering their future employment possibilities; apprenticeships for some but for most via lower-level vocational courses in colleges of further education.[6] The complexities and constant reforms in vocational education from the 1970s are discussed, as are anxieties concerning youth unemployment and young people who are NEETS – not in education, employment or training. When by 2015 all young people will be required to stay in education or training until 18, the notion of NEETS will disappear, most probably leading to further complexities. Middle class avoidance of their children's placement on low-level vocational courses is noted. Chapter 4 records discussions held with a range of people in three local authorities in England who, while influencing the education and training of young people on a daily basis, are still subject to the myriad central government initiatives, legislation and funding decisions. The heads of contrasting schools, further education college principals and staff and local administrators participated in discussion, and discussions were held on new or proposed types of school – studio schools and university technical colleges. Participants accepted that lower attainers and those with learning difficulties and disabilities, now need to be provided with expanded programmes and courses. They were attempting to follow a government agenda which required progression for most students to higher levels or employment, with diminished funding and in competition with other institutions. They mainly viewed current government policies as contributing to a widening of divisions between the academic and vocational.

The book then moves on to examine what is happening to lower attainers and the 'special' in a selection of other developed countries. Chapter 5 contrasts the decentralised structures in the USA with the UK centralised system but notes that the history and treatment of lower attainers and those falling within a special education remit are similar. In the USA students are mainly required to stay in education to 18 and there are more services within schools. The treatment of the groups in question has always, in the USA, been more closely associated with racial issues and discrimination, although here again there are some similarities with the UK. As the Reagan market reforms took root in the 1980s the labour market polarised more, and despite migrant workers taking low-paid jobs the Federal and State governments pressed for all youth to be educated and trained to higher levels. The learning disabled emerged as the largest group of lower attainers, and as in other developed countries, there appeared to be an explosion of dyslexia, autism and a variety of other conditions. The chapter briefly considers the split between special and general education and vocational possibilities for lower attainers. Discussions were held in New York with a university college head of Learning Disability Studies and principals and staff at three schools, and in Los Angeles with heads and staff at four schools, and staff in the Directorate of Special Services. School and college personnel now take it for granted that exclusion from learning and training for both work and social development is no longer acceptable, and there is evidence, as in the UK, that parental fears that their children are losing out in competitive school environments have led to more demands for assistance and resources.

Chapter 6 notes that Germany, like the USA, illustrates a decentralised system where the sixteen states function independently within a wider Federal government. Most states, including the five former East German states, persist with a selective school system post-10 (Gymnasium, Realschule, Hauptschule) although there is some experimentation with comprehensive schools, and around 6 per cent of children are segregated in special schooling. A specific German problem is a partial decline in the dual-system of apprenticeships, organised around part-work and part-schooling, and there has been an expansion of a transition system with various school and college-based programmes now widespread. The continued segregation of children in special schools (defended by a strong special teachers union) and their post-school futures, is now regarded as problematic. Those working with lower attainers accept that most of the students will come from working or non-working class homes, and include minority students, especially Turkish and Kurdish. Discussions were held with the director and staff of large craft and technical college in a large city in North Rhine Westphalia, a Hauptschule attended largely by Muslim students, and three contrasting comprehensive schools. An organisation bringing together projects for migrant and minority young people was visited and discussions held with academics working in the area of vocational and intercultural education and economic expansion. Staff involved with the young people were more likely to make links with the labour market, low wages and the whole economy, rather than, as in England, regarding young lower attainers and their families as deficient.

Chapter 7 explores the issues of lower attainers, those with special needs and their futures on the island of Malta, a small island with a small population located at a strategic point in the Mediterranean. The education system is centralised and heavily influenced both by its colonisation by Britain, and by the powerful presence of the Catholic Church. The economy and politics remain dominated by interfamilial connections and the Minister of Education was accused in 2010 of 'running education like a personal fiefdom' (Bartolo 2010a). The island only gained political independence in 1964, became a republic in 1974 and joined the European Union in 2004. It is one country where there is both a rhetoric and practice geared towards a knowledge economy, as both major political parties committed themselves to embracing new industries and new technologies. But there appears to be little room for lower attainers in the knowledge economy, as unemployment is growing and over 40 per cent of young people leave education and training completely at 16. The system remains selective at 11, although there are attempts to introduce non-selective schooling, and the split between (mainly state-funded) church schools and state schools is predominantly a split between social classes. The state sector is shrinking as more parents 'choose' church schools and there is a predominance of lower attaining students, especially boys, in the state sector. While notionally inclusive education policies are the norm and there are many therapeutic services for those regarded as having special needs, disruptive students are excluded into learning centres. Chapter 8 on Finland provides a contrast, being another country with a small population, but embracing the egalitarian aim of preparing all young people to age 19/20 with educational and skill training that will fit the economy. The Finnish education system has a declared aim of disrupting the transmission of unequal life chances from one generation to the next. The system offers additional educational help in a variety of settings to all young people, some 23 per cent of students being officially given special education. In the OECD comparative international tests of student achievement at 15 (PISA) Finland regularly produces the highest scores, which has led to numbers of educational tourists visiting the country to see how this is done. It is partly due to the lowest 20 per cent of attainers, who attain higher scores than their equivalents in other countries. Nevertheless, the country still experiences similar problems as other countries, especially in the fit between education and the labour market.

The final chapter brings together some conclusions from the above studies. It suggests that the expansion of education to include all lower attaining students, most of whom are now expected to achieve some kind of qualification, join the labour market and contribute to the economy, has increased pressures on schools and colleges in both non-selective and selective systems and in both centralised and decentralised states. As a majority of young people regarded as lower attainers, having learning difficulties, disabilities, or disaffection are now in mainstream schools, the separation of practice and literature on special and mainstream education is becoming difficult to maintain. Structures of separation remain in place and in some cases have increased. The intense pressure on schools has given rise to an expanded and expensive SEN industry, most of it in mainstream schools or in a newer diversity of provision. Political and professional vested interest and parental demand have fuelled the expansion, and governments are increasingly worried about the costs entailed.

While the majority of lower attainers in all the countries studied were from working/non-working class, and minority households, middle-class parents now demand extra resources, anxious that in competitive school and labour markets, their children will lose out. Despite this middle-class parents still avoid vocational courses if possible. A caveat must be that gains from the worldwide disability movement means that many young people with physical and sensory disabilities now have more opportunities for education, training and work experience. In all countries the issues for policy makers, practitioners and administrators are similar, summed up by the question of what to do with lower attaining young people in a global economy, where even low skill jobs now require qualifications. In England there is still a stress on individual educational and skill deficiencies rather than improving the amount and kind of employment available locally and regionally, and a rhetoric linking disadvantaged, non-working families, low attainment and low-level criminality still persists. In the USA with a more individualistic work ethic, and with schools attempting to prepare all young people for post-school college or jobs if possible, there is also an understanding that most jobs will need some kind of credential and the lower attainers may well be employed in low skill low-wage jobs. In Germany the long-standing attention given to vocational education and training makes it easier for government to face the problems of young people in transition to college courses, apprenticeships or work, but the future of those from special schooling remains problematic. Malta is attempting to grapple with issues of school disaffection, dropout after 16 and what to do with lower attainers as the island attempts to join the knowledge economy. Finland devotes resources and an ideology of egalitarianism towards incorporating lower attainers in education, training and employment, and also illustrates the reality that more, if not full, employment is possible if the economy is thriving. Most discussants in this study thought that the notion of a knowledge economy was pointless rhetoric which did not apply to lower attainers, and that attention should be paid to preparing the young people for the lower skill work needed in modern economies and helping them progress in terms of education and skills. There is no shortage of literature on the split between the haves and have-nots in the workplace and the most important issues to emerge centred round how the young people were eventually treated in terms of job security, wages and status. How local, regional and national economies are able to create and sustain jobs and absorb the labour of lower attainers is crucial. If capitalist countries continue to claim the dominance of knowledge economies, more attention must be given to those who will function at the lower end. Among other models which have been suggested to address the issue, a model based on 'flexicurity' for all workers, ending the situation of low wages and insecurity for lower attainers, is possible. Attention could be given to developing an economy which could employ almost all its citizens, including the lower attainers, with more respect and less paternalism or denigration, and also care for those who may not be employable but are still worthy citizens.

Notes

1 I recorded this in my report for the Leverhulme Trust (Tomlinson 2010a). While it was not intended to collect the many and varied insulting descriptions still given to lower class and/or lower-attaining young people, the English media particularly use yob (boy spelt backwards), and chavs (derived from a Romany word and see Jones 2011). NEETS – not in education, employment or training, became a description denigrating many young lower attainers (see House of Commons Children Schools and Families Committee report 2009–2010).
2 There was no formal or structured set of questions provided but participants in discussion were asked how they defined lower attainers, what sort of provision did their institution/authority make for the young people, and what future did they envisage for them.
3 There is a long literature discussing the place of values in sociological and other studies, a consensus being that writers must always make their own value positions clear (see Rex 1979).
4 Of the 193 countries and dependent territories in the world, only a handful would not claim to be capitalist. Even China, with a communist political system, is capitalist in its economic arrangements, although Lauder has suggested that China is in fact a state market economy driven by nationalistic purposes (personal communication).
5 In the UK Coalition Government in 2011, the Prime Minister, Chancellor of the Exchequer, Chief Secretary to the Treasury, and Foreign Secretary, plus the Opposition Leader and Chancellor, had degrees from Oxford University in either History or PPE (politics, philosophy and economics). The Deputy Prime Minister had a degree from Cambridge University in Anthropology.
6 There are some 345 colleges of further education in England, 222 general FE colleges offering vocational and academic courses at all levels for young people post-14 to adults of any age. Ninety-four sixth-form colleges offer academic courses, 16 offer agricultural and land-based courses, 10 are specialist colleges, including those for particular disabilities, and three are arts/design colleges. They are thus separate from higher education although may offer Foundation Degree courses which can be completed at a university.

Chapter 1

Unpicking the global knowledge economy and education

> Upon the speedy provision of elementary education depends our industrial prosperity . . . uneducated labourers are for the most part, unskilled labourers, and if we leave our work-force any longer unskilled, not withstanding their strong sinews and determined energy, they will become over-matched in the competition of the world.
>
> (W.E. Forster, introducing the Education Act of 1870 to the House of Commons. London)

As a background to understanding the place of lower attainers in what is now generally accepted as a global economy, this chapter briefly discusses the meanings and criticisms of globalisation and a global knowledge economy, how education is expected to contribute to this economy and the likely place of lower attainers in an assumed knowledge economy. A section on the English economy and problems of unemployment is included as a preamble to chapters on the various groups regarded as lower attainers and their place in the economy.

Globalisation

There is now a large literature on globalisation, much of it recent, as people try to make sense of the notion that governments of modern nation-states, whatever their political ideologies, believe they cannot survive unless their economies are growing, and in a state of permanent competition with others. Historically globalisation is not a new phenomenon, and links between educated and skilled labour and global economic competition were made in Western countries as the rise of industrial capitalism accelerated, as Member of Parliament Forster noted when UK mass elementary education was ushered in via an 1870 Education Act. In England, towards the end of the nineteenth century, trade with the colonised countries of the British Empire was providing a ready market, and much was made of world economic competitiveness, especially at that time rivalry with Germany, also an industrially-prosperous nation. Rizvi (2007) has argued that contemporary understandings of globalisation grew out of colonial trade, when patterns of integrated markets, financial systems and communications were developing and it was possible to transport goods worldwide. There is now growing awareness that the term refers to increased and often inequitable trade and financial flows, the rise of powerful transnational companies, the speed of information and communication via new technologies, and the movement and migration of people across national borders, with both cultural convergences, for example jeans and Coca-Cola™, and resistance to cultural impositions. Terrorist and criminal threats are also global activities.

The past 30 years have seen the widespread acceptance of beliefs that citizens of nation-states and their governments are beholden to the forces of globalisation and global economic markets. Debates centre on how far governments in nation-states can control their own economies and institutions, but all now adhere to the belief that in developed economies education and skills training is necessary for successful competition in a global economy. Certainly British governments over the past years have used a rhetoric of human capital in which all young people are told that in order to compete in a global job market, they must engage in lifelong learning, continually 'upskilling' themselves to improve both their own economic futures and the national economy. The importance of globalisation to youth labour markets is that within many nation-states, there is a diminishing number of industries oriented to local, regional or even national markets, as transnational business continues to move production across boundaries to where labour is cheaper. Government demands for training and upskilling for many young people become pointless if jobs are not available locally or regionally. National production of goods and financial and commercial activities are now embedded in a worldwide network of economic organisation in which nation states jockey for competitive advantage. While new economies (Castells 1996) may be organised by those who have higher levels of education, technical and financial knowledge, it is the lower-level service and leisure industries, which offer low pay, which are the fastest growing. The concept of a 'reserve army of labour' has been much discussed since Karl Marx referred to this as a way in which capitalists have a pool of cheaper workers (women and children in his day) and can use as few as will make a profit, leading to an 'overworked part of the working class, which swells the reserve army of labour' (Marx 1887: 636). This has become a feature of much modern twenty-first century work for both middle and working classes, where some people work long hours while others are unemployed. The use of migrant labour worldwide, whether or not they take lower wages than native workers, causes discontent in developed countries, although in Marx's time colonial workers laboured overseas. Beck, one of the earliest and more pessimistic writers on globalisation, referred to a 'jobless capitalism' in Western economies, where owners and managers transferred their transnational companies to India and other countries, while sending their own children to prestigious schools in Europe and the USA, and ensuring their employment. Beck described the post-war period from 1945, when Western states provided a measure of democracy, security and economic growth, as a first modernity, now replaced by a second modernity, defined by precarious forms of work, lower wages – especially for the low-skilled – economic and ecological crises and widening inequalities. In the midst of this governments often behave as if it was all out of their control (Beck 2000, 2006).

While there are undoubted benefits from a global economy – for example choice of cheap material goods for Western countries, and employment (even if low waged) in developing countries, there are also increasing social and economic inequalities which have become more and more obvious since the 1980s. Market states encourage economic opportunities by stressing enterprise and human capital development, but incorporate severe penalties for individuals who are losers in the competition for employment and are penalised by reduced welfare benefits (Tomlinson 2005). Among critics of globalisation is Robert Reich, former Economic Advisor to President Clinton, who voiced concerns that once economies were dominated by transnational corporations 'there will be no national economies in the sense we have come to understand them' (Reich 1991: 1). He also worried with some prescience that the rich and rewarded would withdraw into private enclaves and no longer inhabit the same economy as the less fortunate, with those with fewer skills progressively consigned to lower standards of living. Large corporations and global elites benefit, but for lower-level workers insecurity and unemployment threaten. Joseph Stiglitz, former Chief Economist at the World Bank and an advisor to the Clinton government, having observed the consequences of globalisation, criticised his colleagues at the World Bank, the International Monetary Fund and the US Treasury for the ideologies and bad economics which had led to national and global inequalities, mass unemployment and wider social problems. Unregulated markets did not produce either economic efficiency or social justice (Stiglitz 2002, 2007). He was sacked from his World Bank job for his criticisms, although by 2004 the International Labour Office was conceding that globalisation had led to greater social and economic insecurities which governments must address, if stable and productive societies were to be created (ILO 2004). Richard Sennett has drawn attention to the 'spectre of uselessness' which could hang over professional and manual workers alike, as new forms of capital can discard them all, leaving people unemployed in areas in which they are trained. He also drew attention to the worrying consequence of the insecurity of current capitalism, because when whole populations are insecure they project their anxieties onto migrants and foreign workers as a frightening presence, despite their use in labour markets. He noted that 'although in Germany, as in Britain, the bulk of immigrants are tax-paying workers, doing work cleaning hospitals and sweeping streets, which native Britons or Germans eschew, they are demonised as unproductive' (Sennett 2006: 166).

Those who benefit from unequal global markets are, in the second decade of the twenty-first century, becoming more visible as the media and writers seek out individuals and institutions which benefit financially, with rewards often unbeliev-able to ordinary workers. Sklair (2001), described a transnational capitalist class whose members were principal actors in the construction of a global economy. There are no hidden hands in the construction of inequality, instead there are real people who own and control major corporations, media, banks and financial institutions, supported by globalised bureaucrats, technocrats, politicians, lawyers and others who drive the pursuit of commercial success and their own enrichment. There is a global class structure in which highly qualified elites, educated at elite schools and universities, have backgrounds and privileges which guarantees them employment and wealth and are able to reproduce their own children into privilege. More graphically, Rothkopf (2008) estimated that out of a global population of nearly 7 billion, there were some 6,000 individuals who constituted a powerful super-class. Very few women were represented among these 'masters of the universe' but this elite exercised enormous control over the life of millions.

The global knowledge economy

The international acceptance of an entity called a knowledge economy begs a whole series of questions about the many meanings of 'knowledge' in a global economy. As Farrell and Fenwick asked in *Educating the global workforce* (2007), what are the changing kinds of knowledge in different work sectors, how does knowledge become legitimate in these sectors, and 'for that matter, what counts as work in a global economy?' (ibid: 2). The English Department for Education took the view that it was the duty of individuals to achieve at school, train and retrain, skill and upskill and engage in lifelong learning, claiming that 'the global economy has made extinct the notion of a job for life, the imperative now is for employability for life' (DfES/DTI 2003: 15). While philosophers and sociologists have long debated the nature of knowledge, much discussion of a knowledge economy refers to advances in information and communication technologies, especially the speed with which information can be processed and passed around, and increased digitalisation of information (information represented as numbers), leading, as one commentator put it, to 'the selectively increased importance of flows of knowledge and information in some sectors of capitalist economies' (Hudson 2011). Whether it is dramatically different from the accumulation and use of new kinds of knowledge from the mid-eighteenth-century development of industrial economies, is questionable. The brain work required to produce material goods – computers, aircraft, pharmaceuticals – is a further development of nineteenth-century Victorian brain work that produced buildings, bridges, railways and sewage systems, and both past and present developments require physical labour to complete the labour process. What is new is the speed with which information can be passed around the world, and the resulting increase in numbers of people finding employment in new technologies. While on one level a knowledge economy appeared to refer to the newer technical knowledge associated with, for example, ITC, pharmaceuticals, biotechnologies, aerospace engineering and so on, on a lower level it appeared to mean making sure all young people are minimally literate and numerate and can use a computer. Nevertheless commitment to the idea of a knowledge economy, continues to affect western policies. The Organisation for Economic Co-operation and Development (OECD), founded in 1961 to improve the economic and social well-being of people around the world recorded in 2005 that 'European leaders had set the goal for Europe to become the number one knowledge economy . . . with a radial transformation of its economy and modernized social and education systems' (OECD 2005: 3).

Governments of all political persuasions continue to assert that the quality and extent of their education and training systems will shape their country's future prosperity, and it is this belief, as noted in the introduction, that partly underpins the expansion of education systems to include groups who would not previously have merited much educational attention. Nevertheless, despite a growing economy being the holy grail for developed and developing countries, the relationship between education and a growing economy is debatable. Western governments point to successful Asian economies and their higher educational achievements. In fact the economic growth of countries such as Taiwan, Hong Kong-China, and Singapore, was achieved before their citizens demonstrated high educational achievements. Robinson (1997) pointed out that students in Bulgaria and the Slovak Republic did well in maths and science tests but their economies did not exactly prosper, and Marginson (1999) concluded that hopes of national governments that education will create economic prosperity were bound to be disappointed as education and skills training cannot themselves create capital or generate wealth. In England, Wolf (2002) argued that while education does have major economic importance there is no simple direct relationship between the amount of education in a society and its future growth rate, and that an unquestioned belief in the benefits of education had in the UK brought a huge waste of government spending, with failed innovations, revamped and discarded qualifications, and the rise and demise of quangos (see Chapter 4).

New Zealand appeared to be the first country to use the notion of a knowledge economy in communication and financial services, by which it was asserted the country's wealth production would expand,[1] an idea rapidly taken up by other small countries such as Taiwan, Singapore, Finland and Malta. Papers from all political parties in the UK during the 1990s endorsed the notion that the creation and exploitation of high levels of knowledge was essential, in 1998 the DTI produced a paper on '*Our competitive future: building a knowledge-driven economy*' which claimed that all sectors of the economy should be associated with knowledge (DTI 1998). The World Bank told the world in 2003 that 'a knowledge based economy relies primarily on the use of ideas rather than physical abilities, and the application of technology rather than the transformation of raw materials or the exploitation of cheap labour' (World Bank 2003: 1), which may have been news to the millions worldwide still labouring physically and cheaply. Champions and gurus of this new economy rapidly emerged, prominently Charles Leadbetter, who in his book *Living on thin air* (2000) asserted that technology, information, creativity and ingenuity had taken over from physical labour, factories and equipment. He conceded that raw materials and cheap labour did matter, but only gave competitive advantage if overseen by those with high-level ideas and intelligence. This analysis was endorsed by Prime Minister Blair who, together with his successor Gordon Brown, took the view that the economy should be structured around such work as financial transactions, website developers, ITC consultants and creative industries, rather than coal mining, steel working and other manufacturing. The dependence on knowledge-intensive industry certainly rebounded on governments post-2008, and there has been a somewhat desperate rhetoric in the UK that manufacturing industry should be encouraged, and even coal mines opened up, although less discussion of how this should be done. The activities of the highly educated supposedly knowledgeable people in charge of the economy up to the post-2008 recession have not been subject to the scrutiny and blame attached to low-wage workers who relied on debt, or the workless who relied on benefits.

The most devastating critique of the development and consequences of a global knowledge economy has been produced by Brown, Lauder and Ashton (2011). They point out that the neo-liberal 'opportunity bargain' relentlessly peddled by free-market governments, especially in the USA and UK, is now broken. The bargain that more and more education would lead to well-paid jobs, a comfortable lifestyle, and especially if the middle classes paid for and encouraged their children into ever more education, a good job would result. But this no longer holds. Rapidly developing countries can produce the educated brain power at much lower cost in training and wages, than Western countries. The global labour market is now congested with well-educated low-cost workers and the intense competition and financial investment that begins at birth for the best nurseries, schools and universities may be wasted for a majority. As they note 'Today when human knowledge is taught, certified and applied on a scale never before witnessed in human history, the value of human capital is likely to decline' (ibid: 12). The belief in meritocracy is crumbling, as is the 'enduring faith' that a knowledge-driven economy would create ever upward social mobility for Western workers. The encouragement of greed and individual self-interest by governments discouraged people from examining what was actually happening in a global economy, where a global 'war for talent' (ibid: 90) was developing. The global elite and their power, through owning and organising transnational companies to their advantage, has led to a mass degradation of middle-class jobs, while 'many CEOs are now so wealthy that they and their families are immune from the threat of economic destitution' (ibid: 115). But for a majority of middle-class Americans, what was once taken as a normal comfortable life can no longer be taken for granted – something many middle class parents are aware of. In the face of intense competition they have increased their strategies to gain advantages for their children. This includes 'diagnosis shopping' as wealthy parents seek to have their children categorised as having a learning disability (LD) to gain extra time on tests (Brown, Lauder, Ashton 2011 and see Chapter 2 this volume).

Low attainers in a knowledge economy

Low attainers are particularly affected by beliefs that there is a global knowledge economy in which they are unlikely to participate, but it is only when the actual

structure of economies and where jobs have been lost and gained has been analysed that the levels of education and qualifications needed or demanded can be
better understood. Studies generally conclude that in developed countries, technological and communication changes have increased demand for higher-level
skills and diminished demand for lower-level work, and an expanding literature
now discusses how labour markets are polarising (Green, De Hoyes, Jones, Owen
2009, Holmes and Mayhew 2010), but whether there has been an inexorable
shift from physical to mental labour is debatable, as a majority of workers still
carry out physical tasks, especially the 80 million workers in the EU, classed as
unskilled or semi-skilled. In 2007 a British Labour Force survey indicated
that around eight million people were involved in what could be described as
knowledge-intensive work – banking and finance, insurance, higher level IT work,
the established professions such as law and medicine, and newer areas such as
biotechnology and genetic engineering.(Labour Force Survey 2007). However,
that still left over 20 million in jobs which had much continuity with an old
economy. An increase in managers, for example, included managers of
McDonald's™ restaurants, and an increase in small business included a large
increase in hairdressing shops. Call centre staff, telephone sales jobs, nursery and
care staff, teaching assistants, drivers mates, domestic, security and supermarket
staff were all in demand, although gradually rising unemployment affected all
these areas. There was an increasing tendency for employers to demand qualifications for jobs that had not previously required them, and this again was a major
reason for a focus on low attainers. There were also complaints that employers
were taking on the more qualified, even those with degrees, to take jobs formerly
done by the lower skilled, and the kind of work described as low-skill and remunerated by a low wage, varied by local area and region. What was not in doubt
was the continuing connection between lower attainment in education and skill
training, low-skill and low-waged jobs, and in 2010 some 22 per cent of the UK
workforce were in jobs described as low paid (Holmes and Mayhew 2010).

By 2011 national economies in developed countries were largely marked by a
hierarchy of a small superclass and other elites owning or directing capital, well-
qualified groups dependent on their own efforts as professionals or entrepreneurs,
qualified groups in routine jobs, some having served apprenticeships, and lower-
level service jobs, taken by those with few or no skills. The chances of latter
groups finding work depended as much on international, national and regional
capital flows as on their own efforts. If jobs are not available, government policies
to place people in work are pointless, and governments would do better to
interfere and support local and regional labour markets directly than blame
individuals for their lack of skills or motivation. This view was endorsed by a
Russell Sage Foundation review of low-skill work in the USA and the UK, which
concluded that the quality and amount of low-skill low-wage work was more a
matter of national policy than individual effort, despite ideologies of human
capital and constant investment in self (Gautie and Schmitt 2010). By the second
decade of the twenty-first century a consensus was emerging that the labour

market position of the low-skilled was deteriorating. In both the USA and UK around 25 per cent of the workforce are paid poverty wages (Brown, Lauder, Ashton 2011: 116), and welfare benefits are being reduced or disappearing. As Florida had noted in 2002, the low-end, menial job of serving the more fortunate knowledge and creative workers for a minimum wage, offers little more than a 'gruelling struggle for existence' (Florida 2002: 71–74). Those young people who were low attainers and with few qualifications were becoming more marginalized. Yet all were still subject to the rhetoric that in a global knowledge economy all must improve their human capital or face sanctions. The question as to whether and how lower attainers in the global knowledge competition will be incorporated into developed capitalist economies remains open.

The English economy

The UK has a population of some 61 million and within that the population of England is estimated at some 51,446,00. The workforce in 2011 was around 29.09 million, with government estimates of 2.62 million of the adult workforce unemployed, around 1.09 million of these being women. Youth unemployment of 16–24 year olds had risen to some 21.9 per cent unemployed, with fluctuating numbers of these being 16–18 year olds not in employment, education or training (NEETS, see Chapter 4). Trades unions claimed in 2011 that if those not claiming unemployment benefits, those in very short-term jobs and women being forced out of work were taken into account the total unemployed might be double the official total. The economy is capitalist with a mixture of private and public enterprises and institutions, and although increasingly committed to a neo-liberal model of a competitive market economy, still partially retains the post-war beliefs in social welfare benefits for citizens who become unemployed, sick, are disabled, and with child benefits and tax relief for parents. The whole economy has changed dramatically over the past 40 years, as the old industries of coal mining, steel making, textiles, and large areas of manufacturing have disappeared, with much routine work going overseas. The old industries were mainly concentrated in the north and midlands of England, these areas suffered most unemployment. Regional and local differences in work and job opportunities available continue to be an important issue for young people, especially the lower attainers. There has been continuity in some areas of industry – the aerospace and arms industry, motor vehicle and machine tool parts, and chemicals industry, although the large firms are multinational and governments, wedded to deregulation, regard them as largely out of any state control. Some 73 per cent of the workforce is described as being in the service industry although this includes all from highly trained and paid professionals, including bankers and lawyers, to cleaners, care workers, hairdressers and fast-food caterers. Employers in the service area were increasingly using personal characteristics – dress, appearance, politeness and accent – as a proxy for skills. Over half of the top 100 private companies in 2006 comprised service industry, food and drink, retail (including mobile phone and sports and

shoe retailers) travel companies, car dealing and entertainment. The largest
private company in 2006 was Gala Coral, the betting and gaming business, with
Saga, the travel and service provider for the over 50s, being in the top companies.
In extolling high levels of knowledge that new economies need, government
papers usually stopped short of recognising many kinds of knowledge acquired by
lower attainers: presumably officials have never been in a betting shop watching
punters with few qualifications working out the odds on races.

Although around 23 per cent of work is still officially in the manufacturing
sector, the past Labour and present Coalition governments were concerned to
encourage more manufacturing. Prime Minister Brown, in early 2010, asked
'How is the country going to earn over the next ten years, especially in manufacturing?' (Brown 2010). He claimed that the country was a world leader in digital
technology, low-carbon emission technology, biotech industry, pharmaceuticals
and creative industries, and was remarkably positive about an economy that was
in fact already in recession. He did not mention financial and banking services,
which New Labour and previous governments had regarded as so important to
the economy they could operate virtually unregulated, and whose responsibility
for economic problems post-2007 gradually became more obvious – Brown himself having to nationalise several banks. The succeeding government presided over
a shrinking economy still in recession, adopting politics of austerity and cutting
public services and welfare benefits, including those for disability and illness. One
newspaper economics editor wrote in 2009 that

> Britain went into a slump with its economy in a desperate state, when the
> shortfall in manufactured goods dipped below £7 billion the government
> assumed this did not matter because the City, the knowledge economy and
> creative industries would help us pay our way . . . it was total fantasy.
>
> (Elliott 2009)

Numbers of people unable to find full-time work increased from the beginning
of the twenty-first century and after the recession[2] began there was an increase of
40 per cent of those in temporary work unable to find permanent work (IPPR
2009). Women in particular were affected as jobs in public services, which
traditionally employ a majority of women workers, were cut. Both the past and
present governments produced a series of short-term policies in attempts to
reduce unemployment statistics, often adopting dubious measures and with
dubious results. The underlying theme developed early in the decade was that
jobs were available and lack of skills was the problem. A curious document
produced by the Department for Work and Pensions in 2003, *Full employment in
every region*, claimed that 'lack of jobs is not the problem', despite most research
demonstrating that lack of job opportunities in many areas was precisely the
problem (quoted in Little 2009). The paper did single out disabled people, ethnic
minorities and those with few or no qualifications having particular problems in
finding work, and referred to the hidden unemployment among those on

incapacity benefit. A blizzard of policy initiatives aimed at upskilling the workforce followed, a review by Lord Leitch in 2006 claiming to set out a radical vision of what was needed to improve skill training, only asked employers to voluntarily commit to training employees (Leitch 2006).[3] Labour policies which included a Flexible New Deal, a Train to Gain scheme and a Future Jobs Fund were abandoned by the Coalition Government who, in cutting welfare benefits, including incapacity and disability allowances, did follow the New Labour project of a Welfare to Work Programme. This included a payment by results scheme, with private agencies and charities being paid for finding jobs for those unemployed for more than nine months, sector-based work academies for those unemployed for over three months, a mandatory work activity involving unpaid work in the community, and a work experience programme for young people aged 16–24, which included unpaid work (see Chapter 4). These various schemes led to some agencies being paid public money for dubious results, the head of one private company, A4e, paid herself a dividend of £8.6 million while the company was being investigated for fraud (Harris 2012). Coherent government policies aimed at assisting local, and regional economies and helping to create more employment in all sectors of the economy remained limited, and the issue of low wages for low-skill jobs never addressed. In November 2011 the conservative *Daily Mail* newspaper produced a depressing but probably correct headline – 'Double whammy as youth jobless breaks one million barrier and Britain faces chances of a double dip recession' (Dewsbury and Allen 2011). The issue of youth unemployment and efforts to vocationally skill young people, especially the lower attainers, is taken up in Chapter 4.

Notes

1 In fact the New Zealand economy continued to do well via jobs requiring physical skills in agriculture (including beef, sheep, dairy farming and wineries), forestry, chemical and coal mining, as well as health and education, creative jobs and financial services.

2 An economy is officially in recession when there is no growth in that economy in two successive quarters of a year.

3 Lord Leitch, whose report was commissioned by the Blair Government, had past and present jobs which included Chair of the private health company BUPA, non-executive director of Lloyds TSB, former Chair and CEO of Zurich Financial Services, and Chair of the Associations of British Insurers.

Chapter 2

England

Social problems and special needs

> The first and most important thing to do with the backward child is to discover him . . . the defective merge into the dull and the dull into the normal.
>
> (Cyril Burt 1937: 14–15)

Who gets defined as a lower attainer depends on current definitions and expectations of what constitutes adequate attainment in education, which will vary at different historical times, between different countries and between different professions. This chapter begins with a brief discussion of the historical, comparative and current confusion over how to define lower attainers and those with special educational needs, and the explanations for their inability to gain educational credentials. It is certainly the case that as ever-longer education careers and expectations for a majority have developed, the visibility and marginality of those who attain less in education has increased (Richardson and Powell 2011). However, the issue highlighted in this and the following chapter is that almost all young lower attainers, whether acquiring Special Educational Needs (SEN) labels or not, and whether included in mainstream institutions or not, are required to orient themselves to a future of qualifications and work. The chapter notes that in the English education system lower attainers occupy less positive and more punitive attention than higher attainers. A section on the education of the working classes is included, as the one constant, repeated over and over again in research, policy documents and practitioner opinion, is that lower attainers, especially those regarded as having special educational needs, are more generally from working-class backgrounds, and also disproportionately from racial minorities.. The chapter concludes with a discussion of the reasons for the expansion of a special education needs industry, as parents from all social classes become more anxious about their children's future in competitive school and college environments.

Defining the lower attainers

Social class and race have always been essential markers in deciding who was to receive a minimum or an inferior education and thus attain less in terms of currently acceptable qualifications. Historical definitions, especially in Britain and the USA, were based on beliefs in the biological and cultural inferiority of lower social classes and racial groups, and the various kinds of disability and supposed inability within these groups were conflated. In Britain early arguments for offering some education to such socially problematic groups was openly economic. In the late nineteenth century a commission noted that 'The blind, deaf and dumb and the educable class of imbecile, if left uneducated, would become a burden to themselves and a weighty burden to the State' (Egerton Commission 1889: and see appendix 1 for special education categories 1913–2011). By the early twentieth century, eugenic anxieties were centred on groups who might threaten the purity of an assumed white race. In Britain lower class feeble-minded women particularly threatened society by having children – a Report of the Royal Commission on the Care and Control of the Feebleminded (RCCCFM) pointing out that 'they produce degenerate children who threaten the racial stock' (RCCCFM 1908: vol. 1). Enthusiastic eugenicists found much evidence linking feeble-mindedness and low attainments in elementary school to a degenerate social class. Those in this class were likely to become inebriated and unemployed, with delinquent girls in particular becoming 'slaves to their animal spirits' with possible resulting pregnancy (Hurt 1988: 128). Teenage mothers and single parents have continued to be a target for condemnation and welfare reform, with a continued stress on the likely poor educational achievements and possible unemployment or delinquency of children in single-parent families.

Collections of numbers of potential low attainers, either for administrative, financial or teaching purposes, has continued to be a problem. In attempting to sort out candidates for the early special schools in London, one inspector claimed in 1897 that 35 per cent of children in elementary school were lower attainers, 'of every 70 children, 25 were almost entirely ignorant, they misbehaved, learned nothing and truanted' (Tomlinson 2012b: 43), and a Standard 0 class was set up in mainstream schools for those not achieving in the required Standard 1–6 classes. The Chancellor of the Exchequer went on record in 1899, when an Act required local authorities to make provision for defective children, as worrying that too many children would be found who needed funding, an anxiety current in 2012 (see below). In 1984 the then Education Minister Sir Keith Joseph declared that the plight of the bottom 40 per cent was a major scandal in the education system and set up a short-lived Lower Attaining Pupils Programme. An editorial in the *Times Educational Supplement* declared that this number was simply a complement to the top 60 per cent and were those who had nothing to show for their education in the form of certificates. Low attainers in England have continued to be defined as those not achieving constantly expanding qualification levels or required certification. In 2007 a study for the Rowntree Foundation defined low achievers as those who obtained no passes in the GCSE examination at 16 or those who obtained less than a D mark – A* to C being the acceptable level. These students were 'likely to be badly placed in the job market and inadequately prepared for participation in society . . . many of them are at risk of ending up unemployed or even falling into low-level criminal activity' (Cassen and Kingdom 2007: x). In 1996 nearly 65 per cent of young people aged 15–16 did not attain this A*–C level. This fell to just over 51 per cent in 2009, but scores from 1997 were boosted by more vocationally oriented exams which could be counted as equivalent 'subjects' to more conventionally academic subjects (see appendix 2). The Secretary of State for Education announced in 2011 that vocational courses could no longer be equivalent, and that an English Baccalaureate (e-bacc) would be introduced with five specified academic subjects at GCSE level. This will dramatically lower the GCSE attainments of many students and also lower the place of many schools in the football-style league tables by which the Department for Education and the media rank schools every year. It provides an excellent example of the way that qualification levels can be changed in order to exclude large numbers of students from what is currently regarded as the higher attainment levels, and illustrates the point that who is defined as a lower attainer changes with political definitions and expectations. Unsurprisingly, schools serving working class, disadvantaged and special needs students are unlikely to attain these required higher academic levels.

In 1946 some 2 per cent of children were candidates for some kind of segregated special schooling, with a further 8 per cent likely to underachieve but dealt with in mainstream schools. Thirty years later the Warnock Report (DES 1978) claimed those in need of special provision to be 20 per cent, with some 18 per cent to be catered for in mainstream schools. By the late 1990s 3 per cent of children had statements of special educational need entitling them to special provision, but with schools in different areas claiming that any number between 20 and 40 per cent of pupils had learning and behavioural difficulties requiring special help. The connection between disadvantage, learning and behaviour problems continued to be made, with an inspectorate report noting in 2010 that 'pupils currently identified as having special educational needs are disproportionately from disadvantaged backgrounds, are more likely to be absent or excluded from school and to achieve less well than their peers over time' (Ofsted 2010: 5). In its last years in office the Labour government published papers deploring the underperformance in national tests of young people regarded as being disadvantaged[1] (DfCFS 2009) and in particular castigated the underperformance of the 21 per cent of school-aged children currently identified as having special educational needs. Reports on riots in August 2011 in English cities made much of the low educational attainments of those participating in rioting, with one report suggesting schools should face financial penalties for failing to make all their students literate (Communities and Victims Panel 2012).

Difficulties in identifying and counting lower attainers and possible candidates for early exclusion from mainstream education were and continue to be experienced in other developed countries. In the USA in 1909 a school inspector reported that over 33 per cent of elementary school children were retarded (Ayres 1909), and the US Immigration Commission regularly reported foreign arrivals as of low intellectual capacity. In 1912, after some rudimentary 'intelligence' testing, 83 per cent of Jewish immigrants were labelled as feeble-minded (Kamin 1974), and Sarason and Doris (1979) documented in detail the historical definitions of mental retardation and the links with immigration, race, poverty and urbanisation. The wide publicity given to Herrnstein and Murray and their book *The Bell Curve* (1994) indicated that there were continuing beliefs in the likely defects and consequent low attainment of poor white and black young people, with black women who reproduced being singled out as creating an underclass with low intelligence (ibid: 520). By the latter twentieth century around 15 per cent of students overall in the USA, with wide variations between schools and states, were regarded as having a learning disability, and links between lower attainment, race, minority status and poverty continued to be made (Brantlinger 2008, Connor 2008). While there are historical and current differences in defining and counting numbers of lower attainers and those with special needs, the constants are that the young people in question continue to be disproportionately from poor, working class and minority backgrounds and post-school more likely to be neither in education, training or work, or in low-level courses and employment. Low attainments continue to be attributed to deficiencies in individuals and families, with Social Darwinist explanations for the supposed 'lower IQs' of lower socio-economic groups and racial groups still current (Pykett 2008). Denigration of lower-class lower attainers has not been extended to the increasing numbers of middle-class parents claiming that their children have educational difficulties. A hundred years ago the upper and middle classes seldom admitted to having dull, defective or difficult children, but as Tredgold wrote in his influential book on mental deficiency, they did exist but would not need to work or be a burden on the state: 'They can take up poker work, cabinet making, stamp collecting, and participate in the ordinary social amusements of their class' (Tredgold 1908: 145). Now all classes are willing to burden the state with claims for resources.

Changes in the English education system

Over the past 30 years the English education system has moved from being a decentralised system with some democratic accountability via elected local author-ities, to being a heavily centralised system in which a diversity of schools receive their own budgets from central government. They are micro-managed by a centrally directed national curriculum and its assessment, inspected by a semi-privatised inspectorate with punitive measures for school which fail to achieve national targets. A continually expanding collection of diverse schools currently includes some remaining and expanding grammar schools, secondary compre-hensive and primary schools increasingly taking academy status with no connec-tion to the local authority,[2] and a variety of faith schools, with a shrinking number of community comprehensive schools. Local authorities oversee pupil referral units (PRUs) set up to take disengaged or difficult students out of mainstream classes, and although numbers of segregated special schools have declined, policy is directed to increasing numbers of academy schools and 'free' schools set up by parents, faith or community groups, and which can include special schools. There is also a variety of what is now termed alternative provision – placement in educational or training institutions run by public, private and voluntary groups. From 1993 schools could claim to specialise in a particular subject area and gain extra funding from central government and sponsors. These measures have further increased central control via funding, local authorities have gradually had powers and funding stripped away and are left with roles of commissioning services and overseeing school admissions. Currently, some money for special education, school transport and careers advice is still within local authority remit, but a variety of services once provided by the local authorities have been outsourced to private agencies and business entrepreneurs (Tomlinson 2005, Ball 2009). A language and practice of managerialism, accountability, inspection, testing and targets has largely precluded debate about the purpose of education apart from serving the economy, and schools and colleges have become individual businesses.

The previous years (1945–1979) had been characterised by an ideology of social democracy, with a consensus that national and local government should work together to regulate and resource education as a public service, with free secondary and higher education for those qualified. The expansion of education post-Second World War was encouraged by an expanding economy and relatively full and secure employment. The development of comprehensive education from the 1960s appeared to signal a reduction of social class divisions and a somewhat grudging recognition that the working class needed more opportunities in education. From 1979 a radical restructuring of public welfare in Britain began to take place. Reforms towards a market-oriented economy in public services – health, education, housing and other social services – were undertaken by the Conservative Governments of Thatcher and Major, continued under the New Labour Governments of Blair and Brown, and continue under the post-2010 Coalition Government of Conservative and Liberal politicians. Market ideologies, as applied to education, were intended to encourage competition between educational institutions, with new forms of privatisation and private participation in state education being encouraged (Ball 2009). Market states have been defined as competition states or post-welfare societies, and at least one commentator has forecast that in the emerging market states in the West, the days of mass, universal public education, may be numbered (Bobbitt 2002). In England once licence was given for individual and familial advancement in education via 'choice', a scramble for selective schools, or those considered the 'best' in the area intensified. In 2012 parents moving to an area with a high-ranked primary school paid 42 per cent (£91,000) more for a house than the national average. Private schooling flourished, although the recession from 2008 brought some previously fee-paying parents back searching for the best state schools. The accompanying ideology of meritocracy encouraged the winners in the choice lottery to believe their child's success in entry to a good school was due to superior merit, although merit has always been a dubious concept (Young 1958).

What rapidly became clear was that market forces and competition between schools increased polarisation by social class and ethnicity – schools attended by the working classes were never the most popular. Although Western governments had from the 1960s rediscovered poverty and deplored the existence of groups variously described as deprived, disadvantaged, socially excluded, vulnerable and underclass, and put in train various strategies intended to alleviate their plight, there was no abandonment of policies which continued to create poverty, deprivation and polarisation. Extensive research continued to demonstrate that economic inequality is the major cause of a myriad of social disadvantages (Wilkinson and Pickett 2009, Dorling 2010), but governments were more concerned to focus on the supposed individual, familial and educational deficiencies of the poor, than structural policies to reduce economic inequalities. In the public mind a rhetoric of disadvantage, low attainment and social exclusion had become metaphors for crime, antisocial behaviour and educational failure, and many parents became fearful of their children attending schools bearing the marks of low social status and poverty. Thus schools attended by large numbers of low attainers, which in practice usually meant children of the unskilled or unemployed, minority and refugee children, second-language speakers and those known to have special educational needs, were shunned. When suggestions were made that a lottery should determine school admissions, the *Daily Telegraph* newspaper carried an article 'School lotteries hitting middle classes', and deplored the fact that some councils (local authorities) were 'selecting low-ability students or using lotteries in an attempt to break the middle class hold over the most sought after places' (*Daily Telegraph* 2011). Middle class and aspirant parents, in competition states, need social distance from denigrated groups, in ways that Max Weber, explaining the importance of status in communities, would understand.[3]

Working-class education

The derogatory language increasingly used in England to denigrate a variety of groups regarded as members of a residual working or non-working class, the poor, the unemployed, the disabled and young people with low attainments, can be regarded as an extension of nineteenth and twentieth century government and middle class anxieties over the potential violence and amorality of the non-respectable working classes. Metaphors of sewers – the young were pestilence or guttersnipes and wastrels – and the jungle – they were slum monkeys, savage apes (Humphries 1981: 13) – persisted over the century in the various moral panics over youth cultures, especially urban youth. After the arrival of significant groups of minority young people from the 1950s in the UK, the potential for racial confrontations added to political and class anxieties and there was fertile ground for racial slurs and epithets. Jones has documented the freedom with which labels are now openly used, for example, the feral underclass; scum; chavs – 'a term of pure class contempt' (Jones 2011:9); and yobs. The title of this book is taken from headlines in a number of newspapers referring to yobs.[4] An underlying assumption to the insults is that the individuals or groups in question either have little or no educational attainments or work qualifications and have no intention of acquiring them.

The history of the struggle for a national system of education serving working class men, women and children over the last 200 years has been well documented (see for example McCullough 1998, Lawton 2005, Simon 1960). The nineteenth-century education system was designed to reinforce social class distinctions and prevent working-class children receiving an education above their station in life. Eventually some education for the working classes was regarded as necessary not only to improve the economy, as the quote from Forster at the beginning of Chapter 1 indicated, but also to prevent social unrest and even revolution. Representatives of the middle classes, who, in one opinion, 'pass their lives in the steady and unrepining duties of life . . . and know little of the working classes . . . a society of which we are ignorant' (Simon 1960: 345), were usually willing to denigrate the claims of the poorer classes for education, and their children as dirty, irreligious, and ill-disciplined. Eventually economic, social and some degree of human considerations allowed an expanded elementary and later secondary education for both those regarded as the respectable and the undeserving working classes (Simon ibid: 338–363). However the subsequent development of secondary education in England in the early twentieth century was firmly based on a superior education for the upper middle classes in private schools and a hierarchy of fee-paying grammar schools for the middle classes, with a small number of scholarships for 'able' children from the working class, thus limiting much social and occupational mobility. Education for the rest was increasingly to be of an elementary or practical nature, although arguments in favour of expanding secondary education culminated post-1945 into a tripartite system of secondary education into grammar, technical and secondary modern schools. Around 172 technical schools were originally set up but they gradually closed or were incorporated into other institutions.

A selective education system based on social class has provided a useful base for the development of the notion of a knowledge economy. The debates in the 1920s and 1930s, using psychological notions of mental measurement and intelligence quotients, led to serious supposition that young people could be divided into 'Mentals' and 'Manuals', and three types of mind, which conveniently paralleled the three types of secondary school and which gradually became reduced to two types – the academic in private and grammar schools and the practical and manual in secondary modern schools (McCullough 1998: 33). The middle classes dominated among the 20 per cent of students who attended grammar schools, although the movement to non-selective comprehensive schooling in the 1960s was as much due to the anxiety of the middle classes that if their children failed the selective examination they would be forced into secondary modern schools, as to egalitarian beliefs. In these schools the 'ordinary child' would be prepared for skilled or unskilled manual jobs, a fate middle-class families became adept at avoiding, just as they avoided relegation to the more stigmatised kinds of special education. Girls in these modern schools were largely to be prepared for home-making and childcare, although there were some delinquent and immoral girls who wished to 'stay out late, frequent dance halls and coffee bars with boyfriends' (McCullough ibid: 122).

Academic studies from the 1950s worried about the 'educability' of the working classes and whether their family socialisation allowed them to take advantage of opportunities in schooling. Questioning whether working class young people actually wanted much education, especially via studies such as Willis (1977) which suggested that a 'lads' culture rejected what was on offer in schools and reproduced themselves in working class jobs, worried liberal commentators concerned both about economic efficiency, wasting talent and also social justice issues (Brown 1987). Anxiety that white working class achievements might be overtaken by the achievements of some minority children, notably South Asian and Chinese, were eventually expressed by government, supported by some research which quoted low expectations by teachers, economic deprivation, poor housing and low parental education and aspiration as sources of low white attainments (Demie and Lewis 2010). However, with the development of comprehensive schooling – over 90 per cent of young people attending notionally comprehensive schooling by 1990 – the search for a curriculum and schooling which would engage the attention of white and minority working class students persisted, opposed just as persistently by those who believed that early selection for different curricula served class and economic interests better. What was not in doubt was that comprehensive schools increasingly included large numbers of lower-attaining working-class children, who were either regarded as failing to achieve or incapable of achieving required qualifications. From the early 1990s, a commitment to choice, diversity and inclusion in schooling intensified the hierarchy of desirable and less-desirable schools. Desirable schools trained students to obtain the required academic qualifications and led to a place in a desirable university, and which became much sought after with help from money, tutoring and networking. Young people with qualifications from these schools were the future knowledge workers in the knowledge economy. Those schools where young people predominantly progressed to vocational or manual training, and incorporated numbers of children with various special needs, were preparing those regarded as the lower levels of workers in this economy. By the 2000s Labour and later the Coalition Government expressed anxieties that social mobility – movement up the social hierarchy – had stalled and decided that schools taking 'disadvantaged' children – to be identified as whether they were eligible for free schools meals (FSM) – should receive extra money to encourage them to recruit such pupils. In April 2011 a 'pupil premium' was introduced as an incentive for schools, £488 for the first year rising to £600 per pupil in the following year, and initially there was no guidance on how the money should be spent. Eventually the government decided that new measures would be introduced into performance tables to see if deprived pupils were achieving more examination passes. How far schools will be able to improve the test performance of their lower-achieving working-class students is still a research question, and the Institute of Fiscal Studies has expressed doubt as to how much difference the pupil premium will make to social segregation in desirable and less desirable schools (Institute of Fiscal Studies 2010).

The post-war arrival of the children of racial and ethnic minority workers in the English education system was initially regarded as a problem of assimilating the children into the working class, while the parents had high expectations that their children would progress in economic and social terms. Most parents were disappointed in their expectations, although the development of a small minority middle class over the years led to parents joining the quest for the best schools. Black children from the Caribbean were quickly regarded as causing problems for the system and over the years have been over-represented in stigmatised forms of special education, alternative provision and exclusions from school and in criminal records. In 2009 three quarters of young black men born in the country were reportedly on a police database. Asian minorities from the Indian subcontinent fared somewhat better in school with second language issues taken more seriously, although 'whiteness' is still taken as a norm in all social classes (Tomlinson 2008). Any low attainments and unruly behaviour of both white and black working class youth were regarded as particularly problematic. A White Paper which preceded a 2011 Education Act devoted a whole chapter to behaviour, noting that black boys and those on free school meals were more likely to be badly behaved or excluded from school, and teachers were to be given more powers to search students for knives, weapons, drugs, alcohol, stolen property, pornography, tobacco and fireworks, most of these items not generally brought to school by the supposedly well-behaved middle classes (DfE 2010).

It is the case that the histories of working class education usually omit mention of the numbers of children who, once elementary and later secondary schooling became established, were gradually withdrawn into special classes and schools, and defined as defective and dangerous to the social order. The literatures remain separate, which is curious given that it was in the interests of political groups that children who might eventually prove troublesome to society, given the assumed links between defect, crime and unemployment and other social problems, be removed from what was developing as 'normal' education. While, as Cyril Burt and others worried, it was difficult to decide who was defective, educationally subnormal, dull or remedial, disaffected or disruptive, and arguments over where these children should be placed continued, the removal of children into special education developed as a safety valve allowing the smoother development of the normal education system (Tomlinson 2012b: 45). Now, as the section below indicates, the safety valve has blown and lower attainers, with or without designated special educational needs, are regarded as social and educational problems.

The special education industry

Up to the 1980s, it was possible to argue that special education worldwide was an expanding subsection of education systems, rationalised by a seemingly humanitarian ideology of special educational need, which provided a justification for the economic and social position of social groups, and was an important mechanism for differentiating between young people. Its primary purpose was to separate those defined as unable or unwilling to participate in a system designed primarily to produce academic elites and offer those unlikely to be economically profitable or useful in post-industrial societies an inferior education (Tomlinson 1985). Now, this argument needs elaboration. Despite a worldwide movement towards the inclusion of previously excluded groups in mainstream or regular schooling, special education, located in or out of mainstream schools, is a flourishing 'industry'.[5] Special education is no longer a subsystem, but an intrinsic part of mass education systems. Extended institutional arrangements, resources, funding and professional personnel now deal with large numbers of young people described as having special educational needs, learning difficulties, disabilities, disaffection and disengagement. Whether wholly or partly incorporated into mainstream schooling, or in segregated or partially segregated facilities, all are subject to the attentions of an expanding number of special educators, behavioural specialists, psychological, medical, therapeutic and other professionals and practitioners.

An extended literature has, over the past 20 years, debated the practices of inclusion and often deplored the continuation of a special education sector, Slee for example, making a moving plea for the decoupling of inclusive education from special education (Slee 2011: 155). But this is unlikely to happen in the near future. While some regard it as paradoxical that despite there being a worldwide movement towards the inclusion of populations of young people who would previously have been wholly excluded, or placed in segregated settings, special education has expanded, it is in fact quite logical under current circumstances. The more young people are included in what has become highly competitive mainstream schooling, who cannot perform at ever-higher required standards or who disrupt traditional classrooms, the more special education services are required. All young people, whether in mainstream or segregated facilities, are required to demonstrate some level of attainment, and subsequently become economically productive if at all possible (DfCSF 2010). The ideology of a knowledge economy is underpinned by a belief that all groups, whatever their 'abilities' or disabilities, must be educated and trained to at least minimal levels, accompanied by some kind of credentials and qualifications, and not burden the state with welfare demands. The inclusion of more students defined as lower attainers and with special educational needs meant an expansion of professional services to help bring this about.

Governments of all political persuasions, influenced by a variety of economic, professional and parental vested interests, have acquiesced in the expansion of the SEN industry, conceding its importance in dealing with groups who, while being offered some education and training, are in danger of becoming a surplus population in knowledge economies. Politicians have been nervous about examining the expansion of categories of SEN and the many vested interests claiming professional support. One former Shadow Minister of Education remarked that 'we can't do anything about SEN . . . it is a very delicate area' (personal communication). They have deferred to the expansion of interests in special needs, marked by an expansion of associations, institutes and certifying bodies offering certificates and professional development – dyslexia associations being a notable example. A government enquiry into improving parental confidence in the SEN system found parents complaining that their children's dyslexia was not attended to, and promptly promised 4000 more places for training dyslexia teachers (Lamb 2009). Among the proliferation of categories and labels claims came from middle class parents that their children were dyslexic, autistic or had attention deficit hyperactivity disorder (ADHD), and increasingly all social groups began claiming these conditions. Political questions as to why all teachers did not receive adequate training and support in teaching reading were shelved. Dealing with a mix of those who are legally entitled to special educational services and those who are low attainers become a more complex and expensive operation, much of the expansion due to an increased demand for resources from middle class and aspirant groups, many of whose children, as noted, have problems dealing with the increasingly competitive environments in which they are expected to function.

By 2010 some 1.7 million children aged 5–16 were identified as 'having SEN' at a cost of some £5 billion.[6] Following a 2001 Special Education and Disability Act, a Code of Practice attempted to define the responsibility of schools to cater for those with learning difficulties without extra resources and those where parents would get additional help. Thus three categories were developed. School Action, additional school support but no specialist help, School Action Plus, when specialists outside the classroom were consulted, and Statements of Special Educational Need, where interprofessional assessment legally prescribed special educational provision. Some 2.7 per cent of children were 'statemented' with over 18.2 per cent nationally on SEN registers but with wide local variation, in the first two categories. Special Educational Needs Co-ordinators (SENCOs) in schools were expected to take responsibility for these. SEN categorisation has always assumed that there is a normal state by which to measure the abnormal, and historically has always conflated the normative and non-normative conditions (Tomlinson 2012b: 65). There can be some debate but more agreement over normative categories – a physical or sensory disability or severe learning difficulty, but categories of feeble-minded, educable defect, educational subnormality, mild or moderate learning difficulty, specific learning difficulty including dyslexia, maladjusted, behavioural, social and emotional difficulty, autistic spectrum disorders, hyperactivity and conduct disorders, are not and never will be normative categories and there will always be argument over the value judgements implicit in their assessment and 'diagnosis'.

With funding issues overcoming their nervousness, by 2009 politicians from both major parties were voicing concern about the increasing claims for a variety of conditions which apparently required special educational resources. An early review by the Coalition Government noted that some 916,000 children were identified at the 'school action' levels, and promised a radically different system of identifying the SEN. This proposed to abolish the existing stages of support and 'perverse incentives to over-identify children as having SEN' (DfE 2011a: 9), replacing them with one school-based category and an 'Education, Health and Care Plan' for those requiring statutory assessment. This review promised more power to parents in decision making, and reforms are intended to be in place by 2014. Accordingly the Queen announced in her speech at the State Opening of Parliament on 9 May 2012 that her government 'was minded' to improve provision for children with special needs and disabilities, and an Education Bill was promptly produced. This replaced the Statement of Special Educational Needs and the post-16 Learning Disability Allowance with an Education, Health and Care Plan (EHCP), for all aged 0–25 and promised to give parents with these plans control over their children's SEN budget, and proposed removing many children from school special needs registers. The intention was to reduce costs for special educational services and require schools to deal with learning and behavioural problems without extra funding. One result of this will be an increase in litigation as parents make claims if their children do not acquire an EHCP or guaranteed help. The Association of Teachers and Lecturers also immediately noted that teachers relied on specialist services, and that cuts had already affected the employment of professionals such as educational psychologists and speech therapists (Quinn and Malik 2012).

However, it is unlikely that in the near future many professionals dealing with the 'special' will be unemployed. Historically governments have always used medical, psychological and allied professions to support educational and social ideologies, and increasingly depended on these professionals to legitimate strategies to control behaviours considered deviant or disruptive to the smooth running of institutions. These continue to be sought, with a growing use of technological and medical solutions for perceived school problems, especially misbehaviour and disobedience, with 'treatments' including drug therapies, psychotherapy, behavioural modifications and therapeutic counselling (Eccleston and Hayes 2008). Developments in biomedicine and neuroscience have also encouraged government interest in attempts to explain learning problems and deviant behaviour, and research is often disseminated via media quests for 'better brains' (Rose 2005). A UK Parliamentary Cabinet Office Paper in 2008 actually contained an image contrasting a 'normal' brain with an 'emotionally deprived brain' (Cabinet Office 2008: 87). Behind this is the assumption that social and educational systems are permanent and it is the young people who must be transformed to fit in. This continues to cause particular difficulties concerning those who, with more severe intellectual, sensory or physical needs, will never fit in with the work agenda or live independent lives.[7] However, it is post-16 that in England the special needs and the vocational area and the place of the special and lower attainers in the knowledge economy come together, and this will be discussed in the following chapter.

Notes

1 This section refers to policy in England and Wales, although in 1999, after a devolution of government, Wales took control of its own education system. Scotland largely controlled a separate system after the 1945 Education (Scotland) Act and from 1999 the Scottish Parliament controlled its own system, as does Northern Ireland.

2 City Academies made their first appearance in a Learning and Skills Act in 2000, the first three opening in 2002. They were to be directly funded by central government, free from democratic local authority oversight and subsidised by sponsors. Successive governments influenced by the US charter school movement, have encouraged secondary and later primary schools to take academy status, with free schools, special schools and further education colleges now able to become academies.

3 For both Max Weber and Karl Marx, the basic condition of social class was in the unequal distribution of economic power, but Weber developed the notion of status, in which people grouped themselves according to their prestige and way of life (Bendix 1966: 87). Superior social groups need a status distinction between themselves and those regarded as inferior groups.

4 For example (2010) 'Why decent folk deserve better from cops who let yobs run amok', *Daily Mail*, 24 September, or 'Yobs turn park into drinking den', *Evesham Journal*, 26 September 2010 (this article referred to a small number of young people drinking cans of lager in a small country town but otherwise causing no trouble). In May 2012 Prime Minister Cameron announced a scheme for parenting classes 'to stem the tide of child yobbery blighting Britain', *Daily Mail*, 13 May.

5 The term 'SEN industry' was used ironically by a number of administrators of special education services in the research for this book.

6 The current SEN categories in England are illustrated in Appendix 1. In addition, from 2003, when Education and Social Services were restructured and multi-agency services recommended, the DfES drew up a *Common Assessment Framework* (CAF) which identified 23 groups of needs, problems and issues which might affect young people (DfES 2004). These included disruptive or antisocial behaviour, parental conflict/lack of support, risk of offending, school exclusion/poor attendance, experience of bullying, special educational needs, disabilities, disengagement, poor nutrition, ill-health, substance misuse, anxiety/depression, housing issues, pregnancy and parenthood. Other problems included children in care, adopted children, those in youth justice systems, those with English as an additional language, the gifted and talented, white working class boys, and Roma and traveller children. The DfES also drew up an overlapping list of Additional Educational needs with nine categories.

7 Despite a government rhetoric of partnership with parents, those who depend on disabled children's services are aware of a large gap between rhetoric and reality. One mother described by Rogers (2011) reported that she had seen 17 professionals before she lost count, but still had problems accessing services for her child.

Appendix 1 Special education categories 1913–2010

*Statutory categories**			*Descriptive categories non-statutory*		
1913	*1945*	*1970*	*Post-1981*	*2010*	
Idiot	Severely subnormal (SSN)	Educationally subnormal (severe ESNs)	a. Child with learning difficulty (severe) b. Profoundly handicapped	a. Severe learning difficulty (SLD) b. Profound and multiple learning difficulty (PMLD)	
Imbecile Moral imbecile					
Blind	Blind Partially sighted	Blind Partially sighted	Visually impaired	Visual impairment	Multisensory impairment
Deaf	Deaf Partially deaf	Deaf Partially deaf	Hearing impaired	Hearing impairment	
Epileptic	Epileptic	Epileptic			
Mentally defective (feeble-minded)	Educationally subnormal (ESN)	Educationally subnormal (moderate ESN-M)	Child with learning difficulty (mild or moderate)	Moderate learning difficulty (MLD)	
	Maladjusted	Maladjusted	Emotionally and behaviourally disturbed (EBD)	Behavioural, emotional and social difficulty (BESD) Attention deficit hyperactivity disorder (ADHD)	
Physically defective	Physically handicapped	Physically handicapped	Physically handicapped or disabled	Physically disabled	
	Speech defect	Speech defect	Speech defect	Speech, language and communication needs	
	Delicate	Delicate			
	Diabetic	Dyslexic† Autistic†	a. Specific learning difficulty b. Autistic	Specific learning difficulty (SPLD)	
				Autistic spectrum disorder (ASD) Gifted and talented	

* All statutory categories were abolished after the 1981 (Special) Education Act. Children and young people had ‘Special Educational Needs’. Descriptive categories used.

† Recognised as statutory categories in 1970 under a Chronically Sick and Disabled Persons Act.

Appendix 2   GCSE and equivalent attempts and achievements 1995/96–2008/09

		Pupils aged 15 at start of the academic year who did not achieve			
		5+ A*–C grades	*%*	*5+ A*–C grades including English and Mathematics GCSEs*	*%*
1995/96	594,035	329,689	55.5	384,934	64.8
1996/97	586,766	322,134	54.9	377,877	64.4
1997/98	575,210	308,887	53.7	362,382	63.0
1998/99	580,972	302,686	52.1	356,361	61.4
1999/00	580,393	294,839	50.8	348,235	60.0
2000/01	603,318	301,659	50.0	357,767	59.3
2001/02	606,554	293,572	48.4	351,194	57.9
2002/03	622,122	293,019	47.1	361,452	58.1
2003/04	643,560	297,968	46.3	370,047	57.5
2004/05	636,771	278,268	43.7	354,681	55.7
2005/06	648,942	269,310	41.5	354,971	54.7
2006/07	656,396	256,650	39.1	354,453	54.0
2007/08	653,808	230,140	35.2	344,556	52.7
Pupils at the end of Key Stage 4					
2008/09	634,507	190,352	30.0	324,867	51.2

1. Figures for pupils aged 15 at the start of the academic year no longer given after 2007/08.
2. Between 1997 and 2003, an Intermediate GNVQ was equivalent to four GCSEs.
3. From 2003, qualifications such as the BTEC First Diploma were deemed equivalent to four GCSEs.

Source: Adapted from DCSF: GCSE and Equivalent Results in England, 2008/09 (Revised). Table 1: Time series of GCSE and equivalent attempts and achievements. Years: 1995/96–2008/09 (Revised) Coverage: England. http://www.dcsf.gov.uk/rsgateway/DB/SFR/s000909/index.shtml

Chapter 3

England

Endless vocational initiatives

> All must be set to work that are any ways able, and scrutiny should be made
> even among the infirm.
>
> (Mandeville 1714/1988: 267)

While Bernard Mandeville, a philosopher in the early 1700s, would have 'none
neglected that are helpless', his strictures on the need to put all to work, young
and old, able and infirm, could be taken for the philosophy underlying current
government policies towards workers in the UK economy. A major difference was
that Mandeville and some of his contemporaries did not consider that the
labouring poor needed education – literacy was harmful to the working poor,
leading them to become insolent and insubordinate.[1] Now, governments having
decided that the working classes of all abilities are educable, all are expected to
reach minimal levels of literacy, numeracy and some technical mastery. Political
panics over low levels of basic literacy have accompanied the seemingly endless
vocational initiatives designed primarily for young people, but also intended to
improve skill levels in the whole British workforce, and achieve, 'world class skills'
as the Leitch report *Prosperity for all* put it (Leitch 2006). This chapter documents
the vocational initiatives for young people, following a crisis in oil supplies and a
resulting recession in the early 1970s, up to the present time. A variety of work
programmes, which have included young people working for free in supermarkets,
apprenticeship schemes and more further education college courses, are largely
intended as much to compensate for the disappearance of jobs as to upskill the
workforce. The chapter notes the anxiety over the NEETS – young people 16–18
who are not in education, employment or training, although by 2015 all young
people will legally be required to stay in some form of education or training until
18. It notes the policies for those on disability and incapacity and other welfare
benefits, which are designed to encourage them into work by removal of benefits,
and also the increasing hostility towards those perceived to be receiving disability
and other benefits. A review of 14–19 education funded over several years by the
Nuffield Foundation, commented that 'the idea of an educated 14–19 year old
embraces those with special educational needs and disabilities' (Pring, Hayward,

Hodgson, Johnson, Keep, Onancea *et al.* 2009: 113) but had little further to say on the issue; apart from quoting a study based on the long-running Youth Cohort Study which noted that the greater participation of disabled adults in employment and across society made new demands on the 14–19 system. It has already been pointed out that vocational education and training for lower attainers and those regarded as having special educational needs are now regarded as connected. There is also the assumption that the majority of the young people targeted are from working- or non-working-class backgrounds but all are expected to persevere in courses, programmes and training and acquire basic skills and qualifications. The exceptions to this are those middle class and aspirant parents who do not generally envisage their low-attaining children taking low-level vocational courses or low-wage work.

Vocational initiatives post-14

A concern with education post-14 is relatively recent. In 1939, 88 per cent of young people had left school by the age of 14, after 1945 all were required to stay until 15, and in 1972 there was much agonising in schools over raising the school leaving age to 16. It is due to rise again in 2013 to 17 and by 2015 all young people, as in most European countries and the USA, will be required to stay in some form of education or training until 18. The form taken will, if current trends carry on, continue to divide the academic, aimed at those acquiring qualifications for higher education, from those gaining some kind of vocational or technical qualification. These will be either at a relatively high level, through level 3 or 4 courses[2] (see appendix 1), an apprenticeship, or lower-level courses pursued either in colleges of further education, in private provision or in work placements with employers. The term 'vocational education' is itself associated in the public mind with second-class provision, Wolf pointing out in 2002 that it 'refers to courses offered as a lower-prestige alternative to academic secondary schooling and which leads to manual, craft or secretarial jobs' (Wolf 2002: 58). Technical education slots into the hierarchy below academic and above vocational and the absence of technical training has been bemoaned by governments since the 1880s – usually comparing its absence to the technical training long provided in Germany and France. But then, as Wolf also pointed out, much of what went on outside academic schooling, was, from a government and media perspective, for 'other people's children.'(ibid: 59). The divided school structure of grammar and secondary modern schooling was endorsed by the Labour Party post-1945, who, ignoring the irony that during the war young people of supposed low ability had been rapidly trained as skilled workers, took the view that secondary modern schools were to cater for children 'whose future employment will not demand any measure of technical skills or knowledge' (Ministry of Education 1946: 13). Until the 1960s there were no public exams for those leaving secondary modern school at 15, while grammar school students mostly took the O- and A-level exams introduced in 1951 as a leaving certificate or for entry to higher education. In

1959 the Crowther Report argued for an extended general education for all and more technical education (Crowther 1959), and the Beloe Report (1960) recommended a certificate of secondary education (CSE) for the 40 per cent not able to study to O-level and decided that the remaining 40 per cent, including those in special schools, would not require any public examination.

During the 1930s some one-and-a-quarter million students had been studying part-time in existing technical colleges, and post-1945 a small number of technical schools were set up, which gradually disappeared (see Summerfield and Evans 1990). The 1944 Education Act laid a duty on local authorities to provide further education for those over school age, and young people in work could study on day release or full time in the remaining technical and the developing further education colleges. Not much of this provision trained young people to the technical and vocational skill levels provided by other European countries. Apart from any failure to coherently plan for the education and training of the majority of young people who did not attend grammar schools, a further disincentive for not worrying too much about skill levels was that during post-war reconstruction of the economy, employment of all kinds was available for secondary modern leavers, including the lower attainers. It was instructive to note the variety of jobs which were available even for leavers from special schools. A careers report in the City of Birmingham in 1977 noted that:

> The majority of school-leavers from special schools up to 1974 found employment with comparative ease. Those from schools for slow learners had jobs as soon as the term ended. They entered a variety of occupations such as polishing, assembling, machine work, warehouse work, building, packing, canteen and occasionally office work. By 1975 . . . many special school leavers were affected by the recession and those requiring routine or semi-skilled work found it most difficult.
>
> (City of Birmingham 1977)

The pivotal moment when government began to take an interest in vocational education came after 1973, when the price of oil shot up, leading to a recession in Western countries, labour market unrest and the disappearance of many jobs. The collapse of a youth labour market meant an unavoidable focus on what was to happen to those classed as lower attainers. The resulting attention led to industry and employers having more influence than educationalists, with schemes and programmes created and abandoned over the next 40 years, providing a fertile source of employment for civil servants and officials who over the years often moved from directing one scheme to another. This did not prevent what became a persistent denigration of schools and teachers who were blamed for failing to produce the appropriate future worker. In the 1980s a Manpower Services Commission (MSC) was set up to tackle youth unemployment which was then around 20 per cent of young people post-16, and a Youth Opportunities Programme (YOPS) intended to provide pre-vocational training. This morphed into a Youth Training Scheme (YTS) which either placed young people in employment or provided courses for those not ready for work or with learning difficulties. The MSC produced plans for new training initiatives from 1981 and the Technical and Vocational Educational Initiative (TVEI), a technically and vocationally oriented curriculum, was piloted in schools from 1983. Neither Keith Joseph's Lower Attaining Pupils Programme nor TVEI survived the decade. Colleges of further education became more important in providing low-level courses, including those for special schools leavers, and a Further Education Unit in 1979 continued to support pre-vocational education, which included key skills learning and careers guidance. A language of Key Skills, standards, competencies, transferable skills and lifelong learning entered educational discourse. A National Council for Vocational Qualifications (NCVQ) was set up in 1986 and given the task of developing national qualifications. National Vocational Qualifications (NVQs) were to be based on levels of competences in the workplace, and comparisons and attempted 'equivalences' of vocational and academic qualifications became a national headache. It would all have been recognisable to the nineteenth-century novelist Anthony Trollope, who in a burst of irony had one of his characters write that 'the green-grocer's boy should not carry out the cabbages, until his fitness for cabbage-carrying had been ascertained' (Trollope 1858).

In 1988 the O-level exam was replaced by a General Certificate of Secondary Education, and by 1991 the Education and Employment Departments had produced General National Vocational Qualifications (GNVQs), intended to be a halfway house between the academic and vocational. These finally disappeared in 2007, as did an attempt to label them 'applied' O- and A-levels. While important vocational examining bodies had been established in the nineteenth century[3] many occupational groups over the years set up their own, with a Business and Technology Education Council (BTEC) contributing a range of first and national diplomas to be taken in schools, colleges and the workplace. GNVQs and BTEC qualifications were from 1995 accepted as 'equivalents' to traditional school subjects, boosting numbers of GCSE passes for many young people. By 2011 Education Minister Gove decided to put a stop to this and from 2012 'equivalence' would no longer be allowed. This will particularly affect lower attainers in schools and colleges (see Chapter 4). By the 1990s responsibilities for most youth training schemes had been devolved to Training and Enterprise Councils (TECs), employer-dominated regional organisations. These were abolished in 2000 to make way for national and local Learning and Skills Councils, which were duly abolished in 2010 when funding for post-16 courses was passed to central government which allocated funds via a Young People's Learning Agency (YPLA) for those 14–19 (25 for those with learning difficulties) and a Skills Funding Agency for adults. The YPLA lasted less than two years before funding for 16–19 was transferred in April 2012 to an Education Funding Agency, which reported to the Director General of the Department for Education. From the 1990s schools had been allowed to send students aged 14–16 to study part-time in colleges of further education, and in 2010 some 63,000 students

14–16 were studying full or part time in FE colleges. These were usually low attaining or disaffected young people, and funding had been an issue, with schools being expected to pass over money for each student.

There had been a long series of suggestions for a unified curriculum for all to 19 (Finegold, Keep, Milliband 1991) but a review of qualifications for 16–19 year olds (Dearing 1996) appeared to cement the familiar divide, Lord Dearing having been instructed to maintain the rigour of the A-level exam (Tomlinson 1997). After 1997 the New Labour Government continued to promote the view that competitiveness in the world economy depended on individuals improving their human capital, including young people with disabilities and learning difficulties. Leaving education at 16 must pass into history and individuals take responsibility for their own learning. A National Skills Strategy and a Skills Alliance bringing together government, employers, unions and a myriad other 'delivery agencies' were proposed (DfES/DTI 2003) with numerous initiatives and task forces set up (see Tomlinson 2005: 143 for 37 initiatives to 2005). The aim was 'a competitive productive economy which delivers prosperity for all' but the focus for young people was to be on employability for life, not a job for life (ibid: 1). This was accompanied by assertions that a level 2 (GCSE A*–C) was a minimum qualification for employment, which increased anxieties in schools and colleges, many schools focusing on attempting to move students up from D to C levels, with an inevitable neglect of students who could not make these grades. A Connexions Service to guide young people into education or employment had been set up post-2001, a service which worked well, but was severely cut by 2011 when the government asserted that schools should take responsibly for young peoples' careers' guidance, and a National Careers Service for adults was to be set up. An Education Maintenance Allowance (EMA) to assist disadvantaged young people to stay in education and training was given from 2001, with evaluation suggesting that it served poorer young people well (Maguire and Thompson 2006). This was abolished under a government spending review in 2010 despite the Institute of Fiscal Studies estimating that there had been a 7.4 per cent increase in numbers of young men staying in education due to the grant. The removal of services and funding which actually helped young people, plus reductions in funding for colleges of further education (the 345 colleges taking the majority of working class and lower-achieving students on their courses) did not appear to be helpful measures for dealing with a potential workforce.

More reforms and apprenticeships

The New Labour Government after 1997 had continued to assert a commitment to the reform of 14–19 education and training and a series of papers and reports were produced. Under the Blair government, a target of 50 per cent of young people entering university had been envisaged, with one journalist commenting that politicians could not decide whether the aim of education was 'to get as many students as possible into higher education, or to make sure we have enough plumbers' (Crace 2002: 8). A review suggesting a Unified Diploma for all young people at 18 (M. Tomlinson 2004) was immediately rejected by the government and the then Opposition with the familiar objection that it would damage A-levels. Instead more vocational courses were to be available in schools, via 14 new vocational diplomas to be introduced in schools from 2008. These had hardly developed before they too were abolished in 2012. There was a continued assumption that achieving five GCSE A*–C was the benchmark for success, an impossible task for many low attainers. Nevertheless schools whose students did not achieve at least 30 per cent A*–C were regarded as failing, and liable to be placed in a punitive National Challenge programme. By 2008 four pathways had been identified for young people to pursue, GCSE/A-levels, the new diplomas, apprenticeships, and a foundation learning tier. The diplomas, as noted, disappearing quickly, the foundation level was considered appropriate for lower attainers and special schools leavers. It was aimed at giving a progression path to what was termed entry level and level 1 in a qualifications framework, the assumption being that it would engage learners, and increase access to further courses. The website for this level included several pictures of disabled students and a black girl hairdressing a blonde wig. Foundation learners were to be helped into independent living, supported employment, an apprenticeship, lower levels of the GCSE or employment. A revamped National Qualifications Framework and an accompanying Qualification Framework with eight levels appeared in 2009 but it is doubtful whether it was all understood by politicians, let alone the general public. For those wanting information about other qualifications there was a national database of accredited qualifications listing 140 awarding bodies giving out thousands of certificates. These included for example, Mountain Leader Training, the British Institute of Cleaning Services and the Packaging Industry Awarding Body.

While the four pathways became three when the Coalition Government took over, much faith was placed in the creation of apprenticeships. Apprenticeships, dating from the fourteenth century and the earliest form of craft and skill training for young people, had declined over the post-war years, being overtaken by the training schemes described above and with employers becoming less willing to take on many young people. A revival via a scheme for modern apprenticeships was undertaken from 1994 and apprenticeships again formalised as a route to employment. The Labour Government passed an Apprenticeship, Skills, Children and Learning Act in 2009 and announced the creation of a National Apprenticeship Service by which employers were to be funded via the Skills Funding Agency for taking on young people. This quickly developed into a managed programme with over £1.5 billion handed over by government, and was expanded by the Coalition Government promising more apprenticeships for the young unemployed. Apprenticeships varied from the traditional – and usually male-dominated – higher-level training in manufacturing, engineering, plumbing, to new apprenticeships in retail, hair and beauty, IT work, hotel and hospitality. Fuller and Unwin noted the way in which the modern apprenticeships were stratified in terms of social class, gender and ethnicity, and questioned some of the assumptions behind claims made for the training (Fuller and Unwin 2009a), and the expansion quickly led to questions about the nature of the training and employers' intentions. Some employers – a well-known hotel group and some supermarkets for example – claimed to offer short apprenticeships and gave out certificates in 12 weeks, and there were allegations that employers were taking state money to train existing staff (Murray 2012). Fuller and Unwin (2009b) produced a guide for employers and others on the expanding apprenticeship programmes, noting that apprenticeships could be what they termed expansive or restrictive in the training they offered, and unlike the old apprenticeships, there was no guarantee of employment when completed.

Youth unemployment and the NEETS

Historically, having large numbers of people, especially youth, not in work, has been a focus for economic anxiety and even more for political anxiety about the social control of groups with no work or income. The nineteenth century links made between assumed low mental levels, disabilities, little school attainment, poverty, unemployment, criminality and possible state dependency still resonated in the twenty-first century. A report from the International Labour Organisation in 2010 forecast that in developed countries the effects of failing to find a job would be dramatic: 'An inability to find employment creates a sense of uselessness and idleness among young people that can lead to increased crime, mental health problems, violence, conflicts and drug-taking' (ILO 2010: 1).

Despite the plethora of training schemes, and much hand-wringing over a potential 'lost generation', youth unemployment – of those between 16–24 – continued to increase. The various sources of information on numbers of young people out of work – International Labour Force surveys, UK Labour Force surveys, Office for National Statistics counts, Connexions surveys and the statistical data supplied by the Department for Education – all continued to record expanding numbers of unemployed or not in education and training post-16. In 1973 only 30,000 under 20s were recorded as unemployed. By 2010 over 1.2 million and rising were not in employment. Unemployment was highest for those with no qualifications, and although young men were more likely to be unemployed than young women, by 2010 some 46 per cent of young women in the age group were recorded as unemployed, largely due to hotels, retail and tourist businesses shedding workers. The most obvious losers were minority groups, black young people 16–24 having the highest rate of unemployment at 48 per cent, with 31 per cent of Asian and 35 per cent of mixed race young people unemployed. The Co-Director of the Institute for Public Policy Research noted that while those from ethnic minorities and those with few or no qualifications were more likely to become part of a generation lost to unemployment and disadvantage, also noted the drop in numbers in full-time work, as part-time work and under-employment increased – a situation praised as labour market flexibility (Harker 2010).

By the 2000s the government had become anxious that the number of young people leaving school at 16 and not in education, employment or training had remained steady at around 10 per cent of the age group and although the Cabinet Office Social Exclusion Unit was credited with inventing the term in 1992, NEET became a shorthand for describing these young people. The House of Commons Children, Schools and Families Committee, reporting on the NEETs in 2009 noted that 'its use as a noun to refer to a young person can be pejorative and stigmatising, and one witness to their inquiry suggested that it turned young people into an "alien species"' (House of Commons Children, Schools and Families Committee 2009: 8). Media accounts of NEETs usually connected them to an underclass, although there was no evidence that young people themselves were upset by the term or had even heard of it. They might have been more familiar with NED – Non-educated Delinquent, through a film of that title released in 2010.[4] Hayward and his colleagues, in a study for the Rathbone Society and the Nuffield Review of 14–19 education (Hayward, Wilde and Williams 2008, Pring, Hayward, Hodgson, Johnson, Keep, Onancea *et al.* 2009) pointed out that NEET was in fact a residual statistical category counting those left over after other young people had been categorised elsewhere. There were large variations at the local level in numbers of those NEET, and many had been excluded from school or were alienated from the school system They noted that many young people described as NEET often dropped in and out of casual employment or college courses, and could be helped by better careers advice and guidance, others became long-term NEETs with poor prospects, and some were 'de facto' NEETs on programmes but not meaningfully engaged. As with other studies of youth unemployment, Hayward's study pointed out what was becoming obvious – that 'the issues surrounding the NEETS rate are as much a product of long-term structural and economic change' and the loss of jobs, rather than about education and training. This was repeated again by a Commission on Youth Unemployment, set up by the Association of Chief Executives of Voluntary Organisations, whose report asserted that 'the crisis is driven by low levels of demand for labour' and estimated that youth unemployment would cost the economy some £4.8 billion in 2012 (ACEVO 2012).

Yet more reforms and solutions

There has been no shortage of suggested solutions to the issues of youth unemployment, especially 'the forgotten 50 per cent of non-university bound young people' (ACEVO 2012) in terms of their further education, vocational training, and attention from voluntary organisations. Attention increased after August 2011 when rioting broke out in major English cities, a majority of the young people under 19 involved being described as low attainers and unemployed. In sentencing a number of young people, one judge commented that the rioters were mainly 'silly stupid children' but advised one young man that he should feel ashamed as he was 'now counted among the hundreds of yobboes arrested and considered scum by the public' (Ramesh 2011).[5] The previous Labour Government had, in 2009, made a Young Persons Guarantee, promising a job or training for all 18–24-year-olds, and a September Guarantee promising a place in school or college for all 16-year-old leavers. The Coalition Government abandoned these in 2010 and announced a Work Programme and a Youth Contract, with job subsidies and work experience to be provided largely by private business and outsourced from the Department for Work and Pensions to private sector providers. These included the security firm G4S, and the company A4e whose questionable activities were noted in Chapter 2. Employability consultants were to counsel young people and the agency would be paid if the person found and retained a job, again a scheme open to manipulation. In addition, young people on a jobseekers' allowance were to take up obligatory unpaid work experience. A scandal ensued when it became apparent that young people were working unpaid for up to 30 hours per week with the threat of losing benefits, in a variety of well-known businesses, including the supermarkets Tesco, Poundland and Sainsbury's. Eventually most of these businesses pulled out of the schemes (Malik 2011). A further scheme, the Community Action Programme, in which jobseekers could be required to do unpaid work, was also challenged by public interest lawyers, and yet another scandal erupted at the Queen's Diamond Jubilee celebration in June 2012, when a security firm on a government contract brought in unpaid workers to act as stewards (Doward 2012). While reflecting the incapacity of governments to control their national economies, as noted in Chapter 1, the Work Programme could be construed as yet another attempt to recast job losses and failure to find employment as an individual failing rather than a national and global economic issue.

However, in keeping with the strategy that all must work if possible, and as part of the strategy for dealing with the UK national deficit, the Coalition Government also set out plans to reduce the number of people claiming a disability, sickness or incapacity benefit, with the assumption that many claimants could work. From January 2011 no new claims for these benefits could be made, and instead claims must be made for the Employment and Support Allowance. Claimants were subject to an assessment of their fitness for work, with threats of loss of benefits. The assessment process was, in an extraordinary move, outsourced to the French IT company ATOS, and there were immediate concerns over the role of the company and the assessment processes, which awarded points for 'wellness to work'. Eventually the Chief Executive of the panel responsible for monitoring these work assessments resigned, claiming that the 'DWP seems absolutely committed to pushing 11,000 people a week through a flawed system' (Gentleman 2012). Publicity given to disability allowances and the assumption that many were fit for work gave rise to public resentment with an increase in abuse directed at disabled people of all ages, with charities warning that welfare claimants were being portrayed as work-shy scroungers claiming benefits fraudulently (Walker 2012). While disability groups found difficulty in making their views heard by government, some campaigners have found that online campaigns and social networking brings disabled people together to protest at the way the system blames the claimant. One young disabled campaigner set up his own ironically labelled website – www.benefitscroungingscum. Meanwhile in another own goal, the government announced in April 2012 that Remploy factories, set up to employ disabled people with more severe learning difficulties, were to close in order to save money (Ramesh 2012).This move certainly contradicted the faith placed in human capital development and beliefs that 'Arbeit mach Frei' (work makes you free). There continue to be serious issues concerning the place of young people with severe physical and learning difficulties. A democratic society still accepting beliefs in social justice will have to work out how much to spend on helping these young people live independent or supported lives.

Vocational reform again

Although there is little publicity or comment, vocational education for lower attainers and those regarded as having special educational needs come together both post-14 and at 16, although confusion remains over responsibility and funding. Those with statements of SEN are the responsibility of local authorities to age 25, and they may remain in a special school, or progress to a college of further education or a specialist college. In college it is the responsibility of the student to declare they have a learning difficulty or disability (LDD) and colleges are legally required to cater for such students and receive extra funding. Colleges vary in the placement of students with a declared disability as to their course levels and they will usually be indistinguishable from other lower-attaining students at the foundation and level 1 courses (Atkins 2009). Students with more severe disabilities attending specialised colleges had funding passed around over the years from the LSCs to the YPLA and the Skills Funding Agency then back to central government, with funds cut and reliance on charities increasing. The Connexions service, also cut, advised on transition from school to further education or training, although the Public Accounts Commission in 2009 complained that Connexions did not know of the status of a third of young people aged 16–24 with LLD (Public Accounts Committee 2009). School leavers known to be badly behaved or disengaged from education are less likely to be accepted on college courses and more likely to be classed as NEET. Parents of all social classes with children with more severe disabilities were likely to accept specialist college courses or staying in special schools, but middle-class parents were less likely to place their lower-attaining children on vocational college courses.

In yet another attempt to reform vocational education, the Coalition Government commissioned Professor Alison Wolf, a long-standing academic expert in the area (Wolf 2002) to carry out a review of vocational education and make recommendations for the future. This was produced in March 2011 with a government response following swiftly in May 2011. Wolf pointed out that of the two-and-a-half-million young people then aged 14–19, most had taken some form of vocational course before 16 and a majority post-16 were on courses which were wholly or partly vocational, but up to a third of the post-16 courses were low-level and had little labour market value. This was often due to government funding which created 'perverse incentives'. She also noted that at age 18 fewer than half had English and Maths to the required GCSE level. English vocational education was 'extraordinarily complex and opaque by European and international standards' (ibid: 9), and central government's persistent efforts to micromanage the whole system had not helped. She insisted that pre-16 young people should not be tracked irreversibly and only good qualifications – academic and vocational, be acceptable, with no more than 20 per cent of a pupil's timetable at 14 being vocational. Post-16 students should not follow purely vocational courses and those lowest-attaining learners, including those who have LDDs should concentrate on core academic skills and work experience, and the focus should be on employment outcomes rather than on collecting qualifications. The government response contained the familiar rhetoric that pupils should attend excellent schools studying a world-class curriculum, stay in learning to age 18 and have the opportunity to take excellent technical and practical courses. Apart from extolling the best apprenticeships (Rolls Royce and Network Rail being quoted – employers are unlikely to accept lower attainers on these), they agreed the current system was failing too many young people, while taking no responsibility for creating the perverse incentives governments had created over the years. As noted previously, the main response was to remove the equivalence of vocational and academic qualifications at 16, insist all achieve a qualification in English and Maths by 19 and increase the numbers of apprenticeships. Concessions to lower attainers included creating new performance measures for schools and colleges to show how they are helping their lower attainers to progress, promising an evaluation of foundation courses which were apparently too rigid and 'ensuring that schools and colleges are held accountable for helping all their pupils to prepare for success post-16 and beyond' (DfE 2011b).

The Wolf review envisaged a common curriculum up to 16 with some vocational input, but meanwhile, in response to anxieties that many 14-year-olds were disaffected from the traditional schools curriculum, the Labour Government had given its blessing to yet another type of school, the Studio school. A pilot for this type of school was set up in Luton in 2009, associated with the large further education college, and was described in its brochure as 'a new type of learning environment designed to meet the needs of young people who find the current academically focused education system disengaging . . . a Studio school is more suited to practical learners'. The claims were somewhat diminished by a statement that in the pilot 18 young people had achieved an average of nine A*–Cs at GCSE. But the school claimed it would teach enterprise and employability skills, teamwork, communication, resourcefulness decision making and confidence-building. The vocational skills of plumbing, engineering, hospitality and catering, business studies and art and design were mentioned, and all students were to aim for a Certificate in Entrepreneurship and Employability. By March 2010 seven more schools were agreed for age 14–19 students, to offer an enterprise curriculum working with local businesses. The incoming Coalition Government supported the venture as it fitted in well with the creation of a diversity of schools, and a Studio School Trust was set up with Education Minister Gove announcing that he was 'a big fan of Studio Schools' (Studio Schools Trust 2011), and a Division in the Education Department was set up to oversee applications. This Division also took charge of the development of University Technical Colleges (UTCs), an initiative devised by Lord Kenneth Baker and Lord Ron Dearing who set up the Baker-Dearing UTC Trust to develop technical schools for ages 14–19. With cross-party support 12 of these were in development by 2012 with the first due to open in collaboration with Aston University in Birmingham., specialising in engineering, optics, lasers and fluid mechanics. In some ways intended to resurrect the old technical colleges and schools, the UTCs require specialist equipment which most schools lack (Baker-Dearing Educational Trust 2010) and a private UTC opened in 2010, sponsored by a successful engineering firm. As with all new initiatives in England, the current funding arrangements mean that new schools take away students and funding from existing schools.

As this chapter has demonstrated, there has been no shortage of initiatives, programmes, and new courses concerning vocational education, much of it aimed at lower attainers. The following chapter indicates how, in the view of those responsible, this is all working out. The final chapter of the book returns to the relationship between a rhetoric of more education, training and upskilling, and the actual jobs available or envisaged for lower attainers.

Notes

1 One of the contemporaries was Daniel Defoe, who wrote the famous book *Robinson Crusoe* (1724). Defoe did not believe in educating the working class, although in the book after Crusoe had acquired a black servant who did all the work, he taught him a few words of English.

2 The NCVQ decided in 1986 that vocational qualifications should be described in 'levels' with descriptions of the qualifications and certificates at each level. Later 'equivalences' were suggested. Thus Entry level included foundation tier pathways, level one equalled lower grades at GCSE, level 2 GCSE A*-C, level 3 the A level and so on (see Appendix 1).

3 The Royal Society for the Encouragement of Arts, Manufactures and Commerce (RSA) in the eighteenth century and the City and Guilds of London Institute (C and G) in the nineteenth century set vocational examinations early on, as did other chartered occupations, and in 1970 a Business and Technology Education Council (BTEC) was created giving out a range of vocational certificates and diplomas.

4 Director Peter Mullan, whose film *NED* was released in 2010, explained that the term non-educated delinquent has Scottish origins. The film became one in a list known as the British Hooligan Films.

5 Sections of the media were quick to point to the many politicians involved in an expenses scandal in 2009. Michael Gove, Secretary of State for Education, who complained that the rioters had a 'culture of greed and instant gratification', had claimed taxpayers' money for furniture for his house.

Appendix 1 Qualifications table: qualifications with examples

You can see examples of where these and some other qualifications sit in relation to the National Qualifications Framework (NQF) and Qualifications and Curriculum Framework (QCF) in the table provided. There are thousands of qualifications accredited to the NQF and QCF and the examples give only a small sample of qualifications provided.

Level	NQF qualifications	QCF qualifications
	Examples	Examples
Entry	**Entry-level certificates** Skills for life at entry level	**Entry-level VQs** Entry-level awards, certificates and diplomas Foundation learning tier pathways Functional skills at entry level
1	GCSEs graded D–G NVQs at level 1 Key Skills level 1 Skills for life Foundation diploma	**Level 1 VQs** BTEC awards, certificates and diplomas at level 1 Functional skills level 1 Oxford, Cambridge, Royal Society of Arts Examinations (OCR) nationals Foundation learning tier pathways
2	GCSEs graded A*-C NVQs at level 2 Level 2 VQs Key Skills level 2 Skills for life Higher diploma	**Level 2 VQs** BTEC awards, certificates and diplomas at level 2 Functional skills level 2
3	AS/A levels Advanced extension awards International baccalaureate Key Skills level 3 NVQs at level 3 Cambridge international awards Advanced and progression diploma	**Level 3 VQs** BTEC awards, certificates and diplomas at level 3 BTEC nationals OCR nationals

(Continued)

Appendix 1 *(Continued)*

Level	NQF Qualifications Examples	QCF Qualifications Examples		Framework for Higher Education (maintained by the Quality Assurance Agency) Examples
4	NVQs at Level 4 Key Skills Level 4 Certificates of higher education	**Original NQF Level 4***	**Level 4 VQs** BTEC advanced professional awards, certificates and diplomas	Certificates of higher education
5	Higher National Diplomas Other higher diplomas NVQs at Level 4*		**Level 5 VQs** HNCs and HNDs BTEC advanced professional awards, certificates and diplomas	Diplomas of higher education and further education, foundation degrees and higher national diplomas
6	National Diploma in Professional Production Skills NVQs at Level 4*		**Level 6 VQs** BTEC advanced professional awards, certificates and diplomas	Bachelor degrees, graduate certificates and diplomas
7	Postgraduate certificates and diplomas BTEC advanced professional awards, certificates and diplomas fellowships and fellowship diplomas Diploma in Translation NVQs at Level 5*	**Original NQF Level 5***	**Level 7 VQs** Advanced professional awards, certificates and diplomas	Master's degrees, postgraduate certificates and diplomas
8	NVQs at Level 5*		**Level 8 VQs** Awards, certificate and diploma in strategic direction	Doctorates

Source: Office of the Qualifications and Examinations Regulator 2009.

Chapter 4

England

Working with the lower attainers

> English government policy surrounding the 14–19 agenda has consistently used a discourse around opportunity, while placing young people themselves firmly within a deficit model associated with discourses such as socially excluded, disaffected, disadvantaged, non-academic, and having low aspirations.
>
> (Atkins 2010: 253)

Having established that lower attainers in England run from those not attaining the official requirement of five 'good' GCSEs to those regarded as having special educational needs, learning difficulties and disabilities, this chapter records the discussions held with a range of participants who were in influential positions to define and deal with the range of young people, and discuss what they thought the future of lower attainers would be in a global economy. In a small-scale study it was only possible to be selective from the wide range of people who, although influencing the young people on a daily basis, were still subject to the barrage of central government initiatives, legislation and funding changes which have occurred over the years. Discussions were mainly held during the year 2010. In May that year the government changed from New Labour to a Coalition of Conservative and Liberals, with many policies, as noted in the previous chapters, being quickly abandoned by the incoming government, and new policies initiated. Participants in discussion worked in three local authorities, one the county of X, a large rural county with several large towns, one the urban conurbation of Y, and in two colleges of further education, located in county Z, but taking in students from a wide area. Visits were also made to a Studio school in a southern county, and to seminars introducing UTCs. Principals and administrators participating in the discussions were all very well aware of the social class backgrounds of the families and students they served and referred to middle and working class as a main delineator of probable attainments and behaviour of students. In the various institutions visited, students themselves were observed and spoken to informally but not in formal discussion. There is a literature that indicates that many students on vocational courses are misled about the actual opportunities for employment after their low-level courses (Bathmaker 2005, Atkins 2010), and that far from having choice and opportunity they are socially and economically positioned to be denied wider opportunities. There is also evidence that many young people, while keen to work, increasingly find their social identities outside the workplace in social and leisure activities (Ball, Macrae, Maguire 2000, Lawy, Quinn, Dement 2009), although historically this may not be a new occurrence.

The county of X

The county of X is regarded as a very successful county educationally with a majority of schools judged good or outstanding by the inspectorate Ofsted. The elected council had reorganised services, with a Children and Young Persons Directorate responsible for all services relating to children and young people. This Directorate worked with a range of other public, private and voluntary organisations dealing with young people, and had a Children's Plan laying out proposed current and future services which include a Pupil Referral Service for the inclusion and reintegration of young people excluded from schools. The county retains several selective grammar schools which skew the intake of other schools, a number of faith schools, and several schools were at the time in the National Challenge[1] programme requiring them to make sure all students achieved above the 30 per cent gaining the five GCSEs. The County schools with sixth forms (11–18) tend to be in middle class areas but most have links with the local further education colleges. Despite competition between schools, always the bottom line in terms of funding, the Secondary Head Teachers Association encouraged cooperation and partnership which included the 12 special schools in the county. A report produced for the government on the National Challenge Schools concluded that 'there is need to promote partnerships more widely . . . and more broadly to secure better 14–19 collaboration and develop a joint vision and strategy for secondary education'. At this time a major issue debated among heads was the 'equivalence of qualifications' whereby some schools raised their exam scores with subjects that were deemed four GCSE equivalents, for example, music technology, sports science, art and design – an issue which, as the previous chapter noted, was dealt with by the removal of equivalence, which will lower the scores of those schools encouraging more practical courses. Despite the variety of jobs and responsibilities among the discussants, they did, on the whole, see the provision for all young people in the county, including lower attainers, in a positive light, although the government centralisation of education, targets and constant micro-management were a source of discontent. It was noted by several people that the authority was nervous of central government and that many of the innovations forced on schools were 'gimmicks'. The nervousness was related to the fact that funding can be offered or withdrawn on arbitrary criteria, and central government fails to appreciate difficulties in meeting required targets.

The head of a 'successful' school took the view that although his catchment area had changed with more middle class parents moving in, the school was an

11–18 comprehensive school and there to serve all abilities. Most students with the required GCSEs moved to the large sixth form to study for A-levels, but lower achievers were just as important and 'the issue was how to be fair to all abilities'. After a review of the curriculum 14–16 the school intended to develop more vocational courses – BTEC courses in sports, health and social care and tourism were planned but the school had rejected the diplomas the Labour Government had been attempting to popularise. The school had a well-staffed Individual Learning Department and teaching assistants to work with lower achievers. All potential leavers at 16 took life skill, study support and careers guidance classes, and there was a careers teacher and an industry links teacher. In one class of lower achievers discussing their future several already had agreed apprenticeships – two boys in hairdressing and joinery. The school had good links with the local FE college and informed students about college courses especially at foundation and level one for lower attainers. The head noted that with more publicity about the importance of education and qualifications all students were 'getting the idea' that they had to take more courses and examinations, although he worried that it was 'all about a jargon of qualifications and lifelong learning'. Although student behaviour is not a pressing issue in the school, it was not the case that middle-class students were always well behaved!

A head of the school in the National Challenge programme was enthusiastic about his lower attainers, although the arrangements for dealing with them were problematic and attendance was a problem. Unlike in the middle class areas, parents were often reluctant to come to the school and face what they thought of as 'authority figures'. He described his school of 1,200 students in the middle of a large council estate, as a 'large secondary modern school' currently with a small sixth form but with a centre being built for expansion. The school has a number of African Caribbean students who opt to come to his school rather than attend more central schools in the town. Attractions are that the school has technology school status, a performing arts centre, a large playing field and a community centre nearby. The equivalence issue was also at the time problematic and he was sceptical of schools that 'got themselves out of the National Challenge' by offering the four GCSE equivalent subjects, thus raising the school scores. He had an arrangement with the local FE college to take some of his lower attaining 14-year-olds to study vocational courses for up to three days per week but there were problems with travel and transport: 'How can the lower ability, who need a stable environment, travel between school and college and settle in two places?' As with most secondary schools in this county those with behaviour problems were quickly excluded from school. The head noted that exclusion meant that a Statement of Special Educational Needs could be made quickly and either special help provided in the schools or the student transferred to one of the special schools for behavioural, social and emotional difficulties. He was very much aware that his school was educating young people from some working but largely workless families on the estate, and was keen to link with the community to offer services. He recently set up a Trust with other partners and parents to work collaboratively on issues such as adolescent mental health, lifestyles, drug and alcohol abuse and policing of the area. These two contrasting schools were indicative of the educational and social divides that are rhetorically deplored by policy makers.

In discussion with an administrator responsible for working out numbers of places needed for 14–19 young people in the county it was noted that

> the role is a strategic commissioning one, we safeguard the rights of children, the local authority is a guardian of the individual. Schools and colleges are businesses driven by targets and money and targets drive the system. The Conservatives under Mrs Thatcher started all this off and New Labour followed the same path. Schools are in the business of getting young people qualifications and more learners in the school means more money.

Central government grants are made to local authorities who devolve the money to schools, keeping back a proportion for SEN, transport, careers/Connexions and other services. The view was that the grants system was cumbersome and ill-designed. Since the expansion of academies, allocation of funding is difficult as these schools keep a share of money for SEN and other services. Also there were constant changes in funding bodies, the LSC being abolished in 2010 with money coming via the Young Persons Learning Agency for 16–18 and the Skills Funding Agency for over 19. This he considered 'is not sensible, why separate learning at 19, if we believe in lifelong learning'. He also noted that the YPLA (abolished in 2012 and replaced by the Education Funding Agency) had a board appointed by the Secretary of State for Education, and its director was a former civil servant who then went on to head the Education Funding Agency (EFA).[2] He approved of the various partnerships schools, colleges and work-based providers created in the county, although 'there was always tension between partnerships and competition for students'. He defined lower attainers as those not getting the required GCSEs 'which have become the currency', down to the lower levels of non-attainers. 'In any cohort of students, around 25 per cent are low ability, including those formerly classed as ESN. The county has devised another category, MALD – moderate and additional learning difficulty, for those who need special provision.' He regretted that subject-centred GCSEs did not include applied learning, which was what many students wanted, but noted that most of the county schools – even the selective, were devising alternative routes for the lower attainers, although it is still the case that some schools want students who will succeed and 'tell those who will not achieve to go to struggling schools'. The county special schools want more post-16 provision in their schools rather than lose students and funding to FE colleges, and despite the county being high achieving overall, some students still drop out of education each year at 16. Managing transition for lower attainers was a problem, and

> engrained in the thinking is that vocational is not as good as what is called academic and it has to do with social class. There is also the idea of a

knowledge economy, but many young people are not going to fit into higher levels of education. There is also a problem with work-based learning, FE colleges are good at this but now we have lost so much manufacturing employers are not taking on so many students. I am not sure any government is really committed to a 14–19 agenda. MPs of all parties went through academic courses and don't understand the vocational.

Advisers in the Connexions service noted that it had its origins in a 1973 Employment and Training Act, at a time when youth unemployment was first becoming a political anxiety. Careers advice and guidance was to be given to those in education or part-time vocational courses who were not progressing to higher education, to help them decide what employment would be suitable for them. A White Paper Learning to Succeed; a new framework for post-16 learning (DfEE 1999) followed by an Education Act in 2000, set out requirements for this new framework, a number of which changed over the next decade. The new style careers service, named Connexions, survived until the whole service was cut considerably in 2011. Among other tasks Connexions was given the duty of assessing young people with a Statement of SEN in their final year of school and making a transition review, and making learning and support agreements with young people, including the NEET group. In the county the service appeared to be highly valued with Connexions advisors working in all the secondary schools, special schools and three special colleges, and via an online service. The Connexions advisors had strong views on how the service was used, including agreeing with other respondents in this study that the constant changes, abandonment and contradictions in post-14 policy added up to government 'not knowing what it was doing'. In particular the service was instructed to work with disadvantaged and disaffected young people and then criticised for doing this. The advisors were concerned that numbers of those 'diagnosed' with autism and Asperger's syndrome, who were mainly boys, had increased, largely due to parents wanting a medical label 'which absolves them of responsibility', and educational psychologist devising new labels. ADHD still a 'big label' and an ODD label – oppositional defiance disorder – now current. The majority of those labelled as having behavioural, social and emotional disorders were from the working class, especially dysfunctional families who 'can't teach social behaviour', but overall there had been a medicalisation of behaviour, with whole families claiming disorders. In one family even the dog apparently had an anxiety disorder. The advisors noted that under the Foundation Pathways all students post-14 were expected to attend school or college, undertaking work-based training or experience provided by employers or private agencies, but worried that the courses were not flexible:

Many students do not progress as intended and there is a big reduction in jobs for those without training, even though many low attainers have the qualities employers say they want . . . young people who are hard-working, obedient, turn up on time and have a work ethic.

As with other respondents, the Connexions advisors regarded the disappearance of jobs rather than lack of training as being a major issue, with a particular problem being those with mild learning difficulties who take college courses and then cannot find employment. They have recently set up a Learning Disability Support Group to help these young people find employment.

As in other areas of the country, the county had reorganised its services for children and young people regarded as having special educational needs. The organiser for the Special Needs Strategy dealt with SEN students in mainstream, in the special schools,– four of the schools taking children with behavioural, emotional and social difficulties (BESD), and the PRUs. He considered that as the authority was high-performing overall, low attainers 'show up more', especially as they do not get the required qualifications. At this time there were a number of working groups on assessment, resources and the future of special schools and the view was that 'provision of SEN will continue to be important, but with value for money for services being linked to student attainment'. The authority received around £55 million for SEN in the previous year, of which 30 per cent went to special schools, 30 per cent to mainstream and 6 per cent to PRUs. Another 6 per cent went on paying for students at private special schools and on transport costs for students. The educational psychology services cost £2.4 million and the therapeutic services over a half million. In line with national figures, around 18 per cent of students regarded as 'having SEN' were in mainstream schools, 2.7 per cent had a statement and were mainly in special schools. He noted the demand from parents and professionals for Statements – 'Everyone wants a Statement . . . it has become a game', and the county was concerned with the escalating costs of SEN, especially as a majority of the statemented students were in the BESD schools. In comparison with other counties this county places more students in these schools and controlling behaviour by some form of exclusion looms large on the agenda of heads in all schools, with a proliferation of labels – OCD (oppositional conduct disorder) and ODD joining ADHD in popularity. In the county plan for young people, keeping them in their communities for special help works best, especially in working class areas and on estates. He was concerned that low attaining young people should have a pathway post-16 at college that will help them to progress and hoped the Foundation Pathways would help progression to other courses. He noted that one local FE college was taking in a number of students post-14 with plans to increase this provision, but also noted a number of courses that have disappeared or are now to be incorporated into the Foundation Path: E2E, Entry to Employment, being one such course. Places for students excluded from schools and in the PRUs could be commissioned from a range of private providers, and the young people could work for a range of awards, the Award Scheme Development and Accreditation Network (ASDAN) award, NVQs and a Certificate of Personal Effectiveness.

Urban area Y

In this urban area the population was estimated in 2009 as over a million, with 37 per cent below age 24 and non-white minorities making up a third of these. In 30 per cent of households in the area it was estimated that no adult was in work and only 54 per cent of 16–24 year olds were in work. Low attainers and those with designated special educational needs took up a considerable proportion of the city budget. A Children's, Young Persons and Families Directorate included a variety of services for schools and youth, and an integrated services subdivision included a SEN and Disabilities Directorate. This brought together students and school support services, the education psychology service, the special needs assessment service, a behavioural support service, a disabled children's social care team and a common assessment framework team. There was also a 'Language Chief' overseeing those with language and communication difficulties especially in schools with low language skills, and a Disabled Children's Champion. Perhaps unsurprisingly this was all described by several discussants as 'The SEN industry, big business in the city'.

In the central city in 2009 there were community schools, faith schools, foundation schools, recently opened academies, and several grammar schools, which skewed the school entry. Thirty years ago there were 42 special schools in the city, now reduced to 27 and which include schools for the deaf, autistic spectrum disorder, students with profound disability, for mild and moderate disability and for BESD. Several schools have special units attached and there are several separate PRUs. Students with a Statement of special educational needs had priority of entry to schools named on their statement. For students post-16 there are eight further education colleges, several with multiple campuses and two specifically serving students with special needs. All the colleges claim to have policies of inclusion and cater for a wide range of ability, one large college taking students with visual impairment, physical disabilities and mild learning difficulty. The support for students included tutors, learning support assistants, mentors, key workers, dyslexia supporters, counsellors, educational psychologists, medical staff, a benefits advisor and a 'transition to next phase of life' team. The city in the past had a mix of large and small businesses and many lower attainers found work in small firms. Now, according to business experts, although there are many highly skilled workers, unemployment is high and overall skill levels low, and it remains an open question where lower attainers will find work.[3] Among a number of groups advising young people, apart from schools and college advisors and Connexions, are a Central Transition Team, an Employment Strategy Group and a Disability Employment Solutions Group.

An administrator for inclusion and a special needs coordinator working in two schools were sceptical that many lower attainers would achieve sufficiently well to find employment.

> There is a huge group of kids from non-working families, [whose] parents and grandparents have never worked. They can't see the point of school and

soon drop out of anything academic. Many of the low achievers are in need of English language support but there is a shortage of EAL [English as an Additional Language] teachers.

They considered that 'We are extending the SEN label to children who shouldn't get it, they are just lower achievers, often due to family background and language problems.' A Central Transition Team tries to help those going on to college but are hampered by funding rules. They noted one case of a girl with Down's syndrome who after a year at college was now 'back at home with no future, employers are not good at taking on young people with disabilities or even taking them on work placements'. The SENCO noted that most of the students in her schools go on to college but the SEN and lower attainers are put on low-level courses and 'a lot of them become NEETS'. In one school with a large Muslim intake there were worries about girls being taken to Pakistan and not returning to the UK. Other parents are

> vociferous in their demands for their children. They are quite receptive to them having a mild learning difficulty as they know this will bring extra help, but behaviour is often a nightmare. Parents want their children diagnosed as ADHD and given medication.

In the 1990s a forward-looking Chief Education Officer had encouraged partnerships and cooperation between schools which is still evident in the city. A Catholic secondary school visited specialised in maths and computing, and was in several partnerships, including with a special school, and schools tried to share students who were 'behaviourally challenged'. The school is also part of a network of some 20 schools, a large FE college and a sixth-form college and they shared discussion as to the futures of 14–19 year olds. The school mission is for all students to achieve their potential; caters well for higher achievers, and 'for many years we have been recognised for our provision for the weakest and most vulnerable in the community'. Low attainers, including those labelled as having special educational needs, are taught in smaller groups and usually go on to college at 16, but the local special school 'does not agree with inclusion and fights a rearguard action to keep students'. This special school takes about 400 students but the head thinks 'around 200 should be in mainstream. There is no difference between them and the lower end of a comprehensive school.' However he is aware that much depends on parents, some want their child at a special school, preferably with a Statement, some want mainstream school and 'either way there is a passionate lobby of parents and no fine professional judgements'.

An improved school, originally a bilateral school with a grammar and technical track, has a long history of regression and improvement. Up to the 1980s it mainly took in a middle- and lower-middle-class entry, but gradually began to take students from a large nearby council estate. The head, who is passionate about inequality in the society but feels the school cannot change this much, noted that the estate had many families on benefits, and even those households in work were severely disadvantaged. Many homes did not have a computer and parents work unsocial hours. She referred to one mother who will not give her son a house key 'in case he lets his mates in' and so he roams the streets until she gets home. Her philosophy is that every child in the school matters and should be valued for things other than the academic.

> Generally in schools we try to educate as if everyone in the country was in the top 10 per cent academically. But there is a huge majority who would like applied learning, there are practical and visual learners who are not going to sit in classrooms and be traditionally academic. We don't value applied skills and we squander talent.

She had a 'massive group of lower attainers in the school, who do not have a statement of special educational need' and she takes students rejected by other schools who still say 'we don't do SEN'. The school has a curriculum resource centre and a unit for those with autistic spectrum disorders, speech and language problems and ADHD, 'This makes the school a magnet for parents who want labels and resources'. The staff tell her that each year around 25 per cent of the student intake 'have SEN' and mental health issues, and she noted that the middle-class parents insisted on Statements for their children but 'the working classes have no advocates for them'. Nevertheless she was adamant that all children should, if possible, be in mainstream school and thought the local school for mild learning difficulties had too many children who should be in mainstream. She noted the rising importance of qualifications for all 'for economic reasons, nationally and globally', and is frustrated by government innovations which could help but are not thought through. She noted the attempted introduction of diplomas, now abandoned, as she set up an engineering diploma in the school and then had to end it, despite the talk of shortages of engineers. She wanted a curriculum for lower attainers that really engages them and gives employability skills but noted that there also needed to be changes in attitudes. 'A lot of working class people won't take jobs they think are beneath them. In the playground saying "Your Mum's a cleaner" is an insult, and then they grumble about migrant Poles taking jobs.' She has trouble getting students to pick up litter in the playground as they think 'someone else should do this, there needs to be more of a work ethic'.

A third school visited specialised in science and horticulture and was a relatively new build on an open-plan model and well-resourced with greenhouses, allotments and even a roof garden. The intake is around 80 per cent Pakistani students 11–16, plus a large group of Somali students and some refugee children. The school is in an area of the city where people have moved out of inner city wards to more 'respectable' terraced housing with good shops nearby, but the white families in the area are 'mainly those who can't move away and some of these are BNP supporters' (British National Party– a right wing extremist party).

The school audits every student's language skills and EAL teachers separate those with little English from more advanced learners. Due to language and other factors there are large numbers of students with learning difficulties and the deputy head noted 'the usual battles with the local authority to get statements for some children. The authority tries to minimise expense but this is very wrong for some children'. Although the school does not like to label students, the parents want labels and categories. For badly-behaved students there is a Time Out room with a permanent teacher and a team of teaching assistants who target certain children. These do not appreciate being singled out with a 'minder'! The school has a pastoral system which gives more of a family feeling and has reduced bullying and gang culture. A majority of students were described as average and overall the parents are supportive and have high aspirations for their children. The deputy head was angry at the whole system of the A*–C economy at GCSE. In her view 'We have created a monster, all exams and no education'. In 2009, 44 per cent of the students reached the benchmark with English and Maths included and 88 per cent acquired A–Cs made up with the vocational BTEC courses which in future will not be counted as equivalent. The school valued its Connexions advisor and a majority of the students go on at 16 to the nearest FE college, and a few to a sixth-form college out of the city. It was noted that 'many Muslim students don't like travelling and like to stay near their families'.

The colleges

This section describes discussion with staff in four colleges as to how they view and deal with lower attainers and/or students with disabilities, learning difficulties or disruptive behaviour. In the county of X, there is a national college for disabled students, opened in 1967 in an old house outside a large town, as a centre for disabled young people 16–25 to study or be prepared for independent living. Funded by the local authority via the various further education funding bodies but depending also on charitable funding and support from business and 'celebrities', the income in 2008 was £16.4 million and the mission was 'to enable young people with physical and acquired brain injuries for the best that life can offer through innovative, cost-effective programmes of education and training'. Students mainly have mobility problems and a majority have learning and communication difficulties. The college has boarding rooms for 125 students well equipped with the latest technology, kitchens for cooking and independent living, and day students are provided with transport. Around 9 per cent of students are from ethnic minority backgrounds. Staff include teaching, health, occupational therapy, personal and individual mentors. Facilities include swimming and hydrotherapy pools, gym, theatre, art, photography and computer rooms. The young people can study a variety of courses from entry levels to GCSE and a variety of vocationally oriented courses. Few students reach the GCSE A–C level but most progress through courses and some transfer to other further education colleges. A Transition to Leaving Director advises on progression when students finish their courses and the current President of the Student Union was studying for a BTEC first diploma in sports science. Local employers take students on work placements which provides entry to some jobs, although the slightly cynical view is that some employers just want the 'two ticks' for having a positive attitude to disability. Work experience is at local supermarkets, photography and IT firms, the local theatre, arts projects and work with animals. Of 25 leavers in 2009, 17 went into employment, five into voluntary work, one into other further education and one had begun a teacher training course. One young leaver was proud to have obtained a job at an ice rink selling tickets, although being in a wheelchair she regretted she could not skate! The college has a behaviour and emotional support team and 'we spend a lot of time controlling frustration'. The aim of this college is to prepare students who, even 30 years ago, would not have been offered education or training courses with the aim of employment. This fits in with the government agenda of increasing the numbers of disabled people in work rather than on disability benefits. While the long-standing debate on the existence of segregated institutions versus inclusion rumbles on, Oliver and Barnes (2010) noted the equally long-standing criticism that segregated provision does not provide students post-16 with skills and qualifications. This college does attempt to prepare all students for employment, further education or independent living. However, it is still the case that some 1.3 million disabled people have reported that they want to work but often face insurmountable barriers, including the reluctance of employers to consider hiring those with disabilities (Leonard Cheshire Disability Foundation 2009). There is also mounting evidence that public attitudes towards disabled people are hardening, with reports of unpleasant behaviour and severe harassment. In one study nine out of ten young people with learning difficulties or disabilities reported being bullied or harassed (Birrell 2010) .

There are an increasing number of private providers, usually partly funded by local authorities, who take young people who have difficulty fitting into any kind of educational institution. An independent college in Y city, officially registered as a vocational training provider, takes students from 11–19 who have mainly been excluded from schools, including special schools, in surrounding authorities as well as in the city. Some of the students have been young offenders and some have a Statement of special educational need. The director and head, in his own words, 'from a poor Irish background' succeeded in business and decided to start the college partly with his own money and with funding per student from the local authority. In 2010 the college, registered for 100 students, was housed in an old factory near the city centre but was due to move into newer premises. The students were currently mainly aged 15–16, both white and ethnic minority, more boys than girls, and taught in small groups or one-to-one. The deputy head described the students as having ADHD, autism, dyslexia and 85 per cent excluded from other schools due to behavioural problems. 'Many are low achievers and NEETS and the college is good at nurturing these learners back into education and training.' The head's view was that 'unemployment is a big destroyer of lives and I want to see all students get a skill'. The college offers variety of courses in literacy, numeracy, communication, art and design, construction and bricklaying, painting and decorating, from entry levels to level 2, and courses in mechanics and hair and beauty were planned. The head, a former boxer, last year invited a world champion gold medallist to present certificates and awards. Most of the students, coming from very poor homes, were receiving the EMA, money which helped them with travel and food. The head referred to this money as important as it helped students feel they were valued and realise that work can bring in money. As noted, this allowance was discontinued by the incoming Coalition Government. Although most parents are supportive of their children there were problems. Students with a Statement of special need can also claim a disability living allowance and one mother did not want her son to take a job in case he lost benefits. The head's philosophy is that all students should be treated with respect but this must be reciprocated. One boy arrived describing himself as 'the scum of the earth' but later acknowledged that attendance at the college gave him self respect. Overall this college could be described as an institution dealing with an educational underclass who have been rejected by other schools intent on teaching their other students, unimpeded by what Cyril Burt described in 1937 as 'the social problem class'.

The further education college in Z serves small towns and a mainly rural area, but the college principal's view is that there are large sections of the community who have multiple problems with more unemployed families and single parents, who often had few personal or social skills to transmit to their children. The college promotes its strengths in vocational courses and advertises that students spend time in workshops, studios, salons, work placements and practical settings, and that all courses lead to nationally accredited qualifications. These run from the entry level foundation and level 1 courses for lower attainers through to levels 4 and 5, and there was an agreement with a local university for a few students to study to degree level. The college stresses its successful courses in motor vehicle engineering, mechanical engineering and domestic heating and plumbing, and in partnership with local employers there are apprenticeships for students who have GCSE level Maths and English. The principal was clear that the range of abilities of the students ran from:

- 30 per cent who pass GCSE A*–C and can go on to study for A-levels or equivalents.
- 30 per cent are borderline C/D at GCSE level and work to improve scores or take vocational courses.
- 30 per cent are on level 2 programmes but are lower attainers and potentially troublesome in behaviour and attendance.
- 10 per cent are potential NEETs, low attainers, and some who would previously have been classed as ESN/mild or moderate learning difficulty.

In his view the group least well served in his and other colleges are the bottom 40 per cent, and he deplores the 'force-feeding of students into the GCSE machine, which means many arrive at college feeling they have failed, and we have to rebuild their confidence'. The Foundation Skills programme 'encourages students to develop vocational, personal and social skills, improve their English and maths and try a range of practical skills'. These included animal care, land-based and environmental studies, caring and hospitality, computing, construction and hair and beauty courses. There were also courses in retail and business administration, sport and recreation and arts and media. Students can then move on to higher level courses, although lecturers on the foundation programmes were having more problems now finding work placements for their courses. There are few jobs for leavers from the lower levels, and one lecturer thought some employers used Health and Safety regulations as an excuse to avoid taking lower attainers. The Head of the Community Department oversees the foundation skills programmes and students on the courses have a variety of learning difficulties but are mostly keen to attend and complete their courses. There is also a Progression Pathway for young people 14-plus from local schools. These students 'mainly have lower attainments and poor behaviour, the schools want to be rid of them but get credited for any qualification they may get', although 'these students are usually more comfortable in college than schools and most stay on post-16 to take other courses'. Although government funding for colleges is being reduced, the European Social Fund is a source of money for lower attainers who would not otherwise be in education or training.

A view among some staff in the college was that there had been a cultural shift in young people's attitudes and expectations about their future, 'They expect to get money for leisure time, clubs, pubs, socialising with friends, and don't realise someone has to pay. They vaguely expect to get a job, but can't relate this to actually earning.'

Offering courses for lower attainers that would keep them engaged and attending was apparent in another local college in the county, although this college specialised in agriculture, rural and environmental courses, with apprenticeships being offered in agriculture and horticulture, animal welfare, environmental conservation, landscaping, food manufacturing, sport and veterinary nursing. The college had developed a 'Neat Moves' course, which was advertised for students 16–18 not in education, training or employment. Although the course, run by a dedicated tutor, only ran for eight weeks, the students usually moved on to other courses. They came from a wide area, informed about the programme by the Connexions service rather than their schools, and many came from homes with little support, in the worst cases where there had been abuse and neglect. Some students had never travelled on a bus, and the EMA allowance they received plus travel expenses encouraged them to stay at college. On the Neat Moves course students spent half a day out with employers on work experience (pool cleaning, gardening, equine work, etc.) and the tutor spent time helping students with behaviour management and social skills, which included equipping them all with a mobile phone to keep in touch. The course led on to levels 1 and 2 courses and some students found work or an apprenticeship after work experience. The tutor noted that the chances of lower attainers being taken on for work had become more limited since there was intense competition for jobs, 'They are competing for jobs at the supermarket ASDA with unemployed graduates.'

By the end of 2011 government anxiety over the number of NEET young people led to an expansion of the criteria for such courses, now labelled as NEET 4u, and the programmes were expanded to include all young unemployed registered at job centres, those employed without training and those who were in education, employment or training, now labelled as 'EET' who were at risk of dropping out or being made redundant. In addition to an expansion of apprenticeships which colleges were expected to oversee, the expectations and requirements placed on colleges of further education to expand their provision of employability skills training, work experience with employers, working with the unemployed in specific job areas, proliferated. In this county, a Partnership Board Employment Group had developed an Employment Pathway for people with moderate or severe learning disabilities, noting that in 2010 only 7 per cent of those with a learning disability had a paid job. The Pathway group included representatives from the County Council, the local Job Centre Plus, the health and education services and ten charities. The intention was to encourage and help young people from age 13 with disabilities and learning difficulties to plan ahead to eventually find work, and help potential employers understand the problems of the young people. Among other groups helping young people to plan ahead was the Connexions service, now to be known in the county as the 'Support, Guidance and Skills Service'.

Conclusions

This chapter has described in some detail the views of participants in discussions concerning lower attainers in schools and colleges post-14 in England. Questions centred round who were considered to be lower attainers, what is actually happening to them in terms of education and training, and what futures were envisaged for the young people.

There is certainly much evidence that a structural elaboration of the education system is taking place in terms not only via an expanding diversity of schools, colleges, private, charitable and business provision, but also within educational institutions. School and college staff and local administrators accept that lower attainers and those previously excluded or given only minimal education now needed to be provided for in terms of programmes, courses, personnel and resources. Discussants were aware that central government set an ever-changing agenda which had to be adhered to in order to obtain funding and satisfy inspection. They were aware that the central agenda required all courses to be credentialed and provide a qualification that would lead to further progression on courses or into work, although they were dubious that this expansion of credentials would actually lead to employment. Staff were concerned that lower attainers should progress but thought in terms of their destinations being in the local economy. Schools passed on their lower attainers to colleges, some at 14, the majority at 16, and colleges placed them on lower-level courses which in practice could lead to a higher-level course or with luck and cooperation from employers, to a low-level local job. Discussants, with variations depending on the school, college and area described lower attainers on average as around 25–30 per cent of the young population, including many who in the past would have been described as ESN or with a variety of other difficulties and disabilities, who were now included in mainstream schools and colleges and accepted that these groups needed to be credentialed to some level if possible. They were generally angry at the benchmark A*–C requirements, impossible for many young people to achieve, and a GCSE industry which had become a 'monster': not the right direction for many young people. They viewed the removal of vocational equivalence of courses as a backward step, as many students needed more practical and applied learning. There was also an acceptance that physically and sensory disabled students also needed to be credentialed and progress on courses with a view to employment or independent living.

Common to all discussants was the understanding that the majority of low-attaining students came from the lower socio-economic backgrounds, either from working or non-working homes, and were realistic that they were dealing with many poor families in areas where employment was scarce or non-existent. They were also aware that if several generations were not in work and able to hand on a work ethic, this was likely to be caused by wider economic conditions than deficiencies in the families or students themselves. Schools and colleges though, did appear to be taking seriously the task of socialising young people into accepted norms, through personal and social development and teaching social skills. Preparation for lower-level work needed training in skills of self-presentation, time keeping and obedience, as much as higher skills. There was, however, a realisation that young people were being brought up in a climate where leisure and a social life were as important as work, and although more of the young people realised that qualifications and work were necessary to earn money for leisure, many were vague about the connections between work and money. Work, as Lawy and his colleagues noted in their study of young people in jobs without training, was important but it was not the only source of the young people's identity (Lawy, Quinn, Dement 2009). The agenda in schools and colleges was very much concerned with a social control agenda, unacceptable behaviour in schools dealt with by Time Out rooms, PRUs, removal to segregated schools for BESD, straight exclusion and recourse to the rising number of therapeutic and medical professionals. Colleges worked hard to keep all students attending, and many students responded better to a college environment than the traditional school environment. While those dealing with claims for special educational needs were dubious about the rise of the SEN industry, and scornful of the expanding categories and labels, there was an awareness of the increased parental pressures from all social classes for extra resources for their low-achieving children. In the expansion of claims for extra resources and benefits, now a considerable worry to governments, some schools and parents have been considerably aided by the medical, psychological, therapeutic and ancillary professionals who have expanded their areas of expertise via labels, drugs and therapies.

The following chapters are intended to illustrate how lower attainers are defined in a number of other countries, what sort of education and training is offered to the young people post-14, and what sort of futures are envisaged for them. England, as noted, has an education system now intensely centralised, with the Secretary of State for Education ceded more powers than at any time in the history of education in the country. Of the other countries described here, three are largely decentralised and one has a centralised system. As in England, in these countries all lower attainers, whether regarded as having special educational needs, learning difficulties or other disabilities are required to carry on in some form of education or training, acquire credentials and work if possible.

Notes

1 The National Challenge programme was set up in 2008 to attempt to ensure that by 2011 every school in England would have at least 30 per cent of students achieving five good GCSEs. The programme cost £400 million, payments being made for a National Challenge Advisor in each school, with funding sent via the advisors from the central Schools Standards Fund. The 'threat' by central government was that schools not achieving the 30 per cent threshold would be turned into academies and removed from local authority influence. One head teacher commented that programme 'damaged the very children it was intended to help' as by implication children not achieving the grades were labelled as failures (Shepherd 2010).
2 The Chief of the Education Funding Agency was initially employed in the 1980s by the MSC, moving to a merged Department of Education and Employment in the 1990s, then to the DfCSF as a 'Director of Local Transformations', then on to lead the YPLA and then the EFA, illustrating the point that over the years changes in the quasi-government agencies provided good employment for civil servants (Murray 2011).
3 The Regional Development Agency for the Area (abolished 2010) had identified clusters of employment for development which included automotive engineering, aerospace, building and environment technologies, ICT, interiors and design, medical technologies, rail, screen and sound, business and professional services, tourism and leisure, arts and the creative industry.

Chapter 5

USA

Divergence by race

Much of the empirical research . . . explores patterns of over-representation of minority children by disability category and whether, once identified, they experience relatively less access to the general education classroom than similarly situated white children. The evidence suggests that Black over-representation is substantial in state after state.

(Losen and Orfield 2010: xvii)

The decentralised structure in the USA, where the Federal Government sets a framework within which the 50 states function, but largely delegates educational control to states and then to local school districts and boards, provides a contrast to the UK centralised system where local authorities have progressively lost decision-making and funding powers. Nevertheless, the history and treatment of lower attainers and those falling within categories of disability and special education are remarkably similar in the two countries. External economic, political and social factors and internal pressures from teachers and parents, ensured the development of an expanding special education sector dealing with the disabled, the disruptive and lower attainers. Compulsory attendance laws in the nineteenth century brought a variety of unwelcome children into the public school system, mainly those from poor homes, the immigrant and foreign-born. Truants, incorrigibles, cripples, the deaf, those with visual and speech defects, the mentally deficient, the feeble-minded and moral delinquents were all candidates for exclusion from public schools or regular classes. 'In regular grades the feeble-minded and subnormal represent an unassimilable accumulation of human clinkers, ballast, driftwood, or derelicts that seriously retard the progress of the entire class and constitute a positive irritant to the teachers and other pupils' (Wallin 1924, quoted in Laserson 1983: 23).[1] As in the UK teachers were expected to credential young people to levels where they could function to arbitrary required levels, and those who impeded this were candidates for removal from regular schooling and regarded as a 'surplus population' in the labour market. As in England social class and race were markers in deciding who should receive an inferior education, and in both countries this was based on beliefs in the biological and cultural inferiority of lower social classes and racial groups. While these beliefs still persist in both countries, education in the USA is strongly influenced by persistent beliefs that racial minorities are likely to be less educable, and a large literature continues to indicate that minorities are more likely to be considered lower attainers. As Blanchett noted:

> It is no secret that African Americans and other students of colour, a disproportionate percentage of whom live in poverty and are educated in urban schools, have experienced educational inequities for decades while their white peers have received a higher quality education.
>
> (Blanchett 2008: foreword)

As in the UK, parental anxieties have intensified as educational attainment has become more important to gain any kind of job, and an expanding SEN industry is additionally fuelled by middle class parents now seeking extra help and resources for their children.

The USA is still the world's largest economy, and of the top world 500 companies, 133 have headquarters in the country. Out of a workforce of some 154.4 million, 9.4 per cent were unemployed in 2009 with youth unemployment of 16–24 year olds being 18.5 per cent of the potential workforce. Disadvantages by race show up in unemployment figures, with 8.5 per cent of white young people likely to be unemployed compared to 35.5 per cent of African Americans, 20 per cent Hispanic and 15 per cent Asian young people. In common with other countries, as the twentieth century progressed the demands of a global economy meant that youth populations could not be ignored and if possible all young people be trained to fit in with local and national economies, although as the Reagan market reforms took shape during the 1980s the labour market polarised more sharply into higher-skilled jobs and lower-skilled low-paid jobs. While economic analyses generally concluded that it was migrant workers, black, Hispanic and other minorities, and women in all groups who took lower-wage jobs, government was pressured by economic and human rights agendas to concede that all potential lower-skilled young workers needed more education. Educating lower attainers of all descriptions became big business both for Federal and State Governments and private sector interests.

Sleeter (1986,1987) was one of the first scholars to argue that while the emerging category of learning disability initially allowed white middle-class parents to separate their low-attaining children from working class and racial minorities, it was the economic and military expansion during the cold war competition with the USSR in the 1960s that led to demands for schools to raise educational standards overall. More recent Federal requirements to raise standards, exemplified by the Bush government's 'No Child left Behind' Act (Hall and Parker 2007) and the Obama 'Race to the Top' initiative (*The Economist* 2009), has increased the need for protection from the pressures of 'raised standards' requirements. The demand for special education resources and exemptions, not only from white but also minority middle-class parents, with an escalation of categories, and litigation if demands are not met, has been evident for some time (Callahan 2004). As in England, schools and teachers were blamed if arbitrary requirements were not satisfied. While many schools and teachers struggled to fulfil what were often impossible demands, counter strategies by local districts, teachers and their unions quickly developed (Lipman 2004, Hursh 2005). The expansion of the 'SEN industry' became an important palliative for schools as well as parents, and provided much employment for a range of professionals (Brantlinger 2008). This chapter documents the expansion of special education, the vocational education available for young lower attainers, and the views of participants in discussions in New York and Los Angeles schools and administrations. It mainly refers to those in what became known as 'high-incidence' categories, those covering the majority of young people assessed as learning disabled and/or with behavioural issues, who, as in other countries, merge with those lower-attaining students without a 'diagnosis' or who have dropped out of school.[2]

The learning disabled and other negatives

A major difference with the UK is that although in the USA there is still an official school leaving age of 16/17 it is the norm for most students to stay in public or private high school until 18 or 19, with expectations that, apart from drop-outs and removals, all will progress to at least a two-year, and preferably a four-year college/university course or find employment. There is no agonising about a 'NEET generation' between 16–18, but in high schools, attention is given to the transition of lower-attaining young people from 14–15, to some kind of vocationally-oriented course, preferably with work experience, which will lead on to some kind of post-school or college course or employment. The majority of these low-attaining students are described as having a learning disability and have the required Individual Education Programme (IEP). As in England categories of special education developed from the late-nineteenth and early-twentieth century in response to children who were troublesome to schools and society, with the familiar assumed links between defects, low attainment, unemployment, crime, pauperism and prostitution. Richardson and Powell (2011) and Powell (2010 and see Appendix 1) illustrate the categories of special education developed in the USA between 1920 and 2005, which are similar to English categories, and in both countries categorisation was heavily dependent on medical and psychological models and influence. In their extensive comparative discussion of the origins and development of special education, Richardson and Powell noted that the whole edifice of special education and its ever-changing population of young people, cannot be understood without reference to vocational education and labour markets, and also to ethnic stratification, family contexts and delinquency, but in the USA as in other countries, there is a persistent separation between special and general education and a lack of connection with other social institutions.[3] In particular there is a lack of connection with labour markets and questioning what kind of future schools and colleges are preparing the special and lower attainers for. There is a political reluctance to accept that Federal mandates to raise standards and expect schools to focus on a 'core curriculum' will lead to more parental demands for resources and extra help for their children in the increasingly competitive educational environment. The expansion of special educational services, in turn, serves the expanding vested interest of medical, psychological, therapeutic and other services which results in vastly increased expenditure for government at all levels. Practitioners searching for improved teaching methods to prevent school failure do not have political support – governments, as noted, finding it easier to blame young people, schools and teachers for failure than adopt egalitarian methods of preventing failure (see Chapter 8).

As in England the largest number of young people regarded as having learning difficulties and unacceptable school behaviour were always largely working class, male and minority, and likely to be placed in more stigmatised kinds of special education, although those with severe intellectual and physical disabilities – the 'low-incidence' – came from all social classes and parents were unlikely to challenge their special educational placements. In England from the 1960s black parents objected to their children being labelled as educationally subnormal (ESN) and in the USA black parents took issue with their children being labelled as educably mentally retarded (EMR). These parents were eventually successful in using litigation to have their children reclassified, and the learning disability (LD) category now includes black, Hispanic and other minority students. Sleeter noted that LD was first presented as an offshoot of medical brain research, with psychologists, neurologists and medical practitioners explaining difficulties in acquiring reading, writing and number skills as due to 'minimal brain dysfunction' (Sleeter 1986), which became a very popular explanation. Sigmon (1990: 35) noted that 'it is extraordinary that a notion so diffuse as learning disability has become a major focus for contemporary special education in such a short period of time'. One of the early attractions of the category was the use of dubious IQ testing methods to suggest that failing white middle-class students 'really' belonged to higher school tracks and not in stigmatised special education categories. This is similar to the later rise in the category of dyslexia where sufferers can claim a higher IQ despite their difficulties in acquiring literacy skills. The Federal Government currently defines learning disability as 'a disorder in one or more of the basic psychological processes involved in or using language, spoken or written, which disorder may manifest itself in imperfect ability to listen, think, speak, write, spell, or do mathematical calculations' (Individuals with Disabilities Act 2004, 20 USC: 1410–30). In contrast to England, LD was not intended to cover learning problems connected to physical or sensory conditions, or emotional, cultural or economic disadvantage. In both countries, however, there are problems in deciding what the origins of a learning difficulty are, and Connor (2008) has pointed out that the multiple and competing theories suggested usually describe what LD is 'not'. What is clear, however, is that for white suburban and middle class students, an LD diagnosis brings extra service support in general classrooms and accommodation in high-status examinations, while for Black, Latino, urban, working class or poor it signifies decreased access to general education and more restrictive placements.

(Connor 2008: 15)

Nevertheless, as Varenne and McDermott pointed out in 1999, LD is now institutionalised in the USA as a crucial part of the education system. In competitive cultures testing and grading is designed to discover *Successful failure* (Varenne and McDermott 1999), and the category both acts as a palliative and provides expensive hope that failure can be rectified. 'One thing LD people have in common is that of average or above average intelligence . . . they are not just dumb or stupid' (Parzych 1997: 4). This publication reassures those with the label that many well-known people have suffered or suffer from 'mixing up words and letters when reading'. Examples given are Albert Einstein, Thomas Edison, Leonardi da Vinci, August Rodin, Stevie Wonder, Tom Cruise and Whoopi Goldberg.

The dominance of the medical profession in the assessment and treatment of defect and disability from the nineteenth century, and the influence of psychologists and techniques of mental measurement from the early twentieth, have been well documented, with continued battles for control over definitions, causes and procedures between professions (Gould 1981, Tomlinson 1996, Oliver 1990). Historically and currently governments have used medical, psychological and allied professionals to support educational and social ideologies, and strategies to control deviant behaviour continue to be sought. In the USA in 1975 Schrag and Divoky wrote perceptively about the growing use of medical and techno-logical solutions for perceived educational problems. School misbehaviour, disobedience and disaffection were to be treated in various ways including drug therapy, psychotherapy, behaviour modification and even brain surgery. Among what became regarded as specific disorders – hyperactivity, later ADHD, emotional disorders, conduct disorders, autistic spectrum disorders, oppositional conduct disorders – all were candidates for medical and allied professional interven-tion. Social and educational systems were regarded as permanent and legitimate and 'it was the individual who had to be transformed if he was unable to live within it' (Schrag and Divoky 1975: 50). While there is considerable evidence for an increase in the use of drugs to control school behaviour, profes-sional neuroscientists now make claims in advances for understanding the relationships between neural development, learning capacities and disruptive behaviour. Indeed Rose, himself a neuroscientist, has described the 'increasingly imperialising claims' of neuroscientists whose research is often disseminated via media quests for 'better brains' (Rose 2005: vii). However, whatever the assumed brain capacity, all young people are now, if possible, to be prepared for a future of work.

Vocational education

In the USA what is termed vocational education varies between states, although the Smith-Hughes Act of 1917 ensured that the Federal Government would oversee and provide some funding for vocational courses. These were to be primarily in public high schools to prevent an academic–vocational split and would help schools retain less academic students. In the early twentieth century some attempts were made to introduce German-style apprenticeships, but, unlike in Germany, employers, unions and educationalists never worked harmoniously together agreeing on aims and outcomes. In 1973 a Vocational Rehabilitation Act prohibited discrimination against individuals with disabilities, and in 1984 the Carl-Perkins Education Act (extended in 1990) increased Federal support for vocational education in schools. Supported by Federal money a variety of School-to-Work programmes developed which included the provision of motor vehicle repair shops, metal and woodwork courses, business and home economics courses. The tracking of lower-attaining working-class and minority students into these programmes has been well documented (Oakes 1985, Weiss 1990, Lipman 2004). What has been described as an 'economising of education' meant more attention being given to school-to-work and vocational programmes and there was greater recognition of changing workplace practices, centred round the production of flexible workers and adapting to a split labour market of high- and low-skill jobs. A report for the Commercial Club of Chicago in 1998 noted that while more skilled workers were needed, the new economy also required people who could simply read instruction manuals and had basic maths and literacy skills. Minorities in low-performing schools were likely to form a large part of the low-skill workforce but would need these basic skills (Johnson 1998).

While there are still small numbers of technical and trade schools for students and adults post-16, and apprenticeships in some trades, it is largely the two-year state community colleges which provide around 30 per cent of the nation's vocational education and training after high school, with private colleges providing the bulk of post-secondary vocational and career training, including military and technical training. Private vocational colleges offer degree-oriented courses in 'high growth' occupational areas – accounting, business, IT, paralegal, criminal justice, medial and dental assistance, health related, fashion, sales and multimedia – and lower attainers can progress to these levels with adequate previous qualifications and money for fees. There are some suggestions that the classic American Dream of a college degree for all, may be becoming less necessary in the current economic climate, and entry-level employment or an apprenticeship provide a better rate of return for young people, especially for those who drop out of college courses (Steinberg 2010). These suggestions have been countered by those who note that it is black and Hispanic students who drop out more and that this could be another way of creating unequal opportunities. Lipman has pointed out that a differentiated school and college curriculum has acquired a new significance in economies where vocational education is not high status and 'in the informational economy one's education is a key determinant of whether one will be a high paid knowledge worker or part of the down-graded sector of labour' (Lipman 2004: 63). While she does not suggest a simple correspondence between school and the workforce, she does note that closer links between education and the economy is creating a system that is less inclusive, more selective and reproduces a differentiated workforce. But the workforce must be trained, and with much variation most states have developed special support services, transition services, rehabilitation departments, occupational and skills training centres, job centres, employment development centres and other services to support low-attaining young people, especially those with disabilities and learning difficulties, to find employment if possible. The oldest and largest federally funded job training and education for 'economically disadvantaged youth' – the Job Corps, was established in 1964 and has centres in 48 states providing training, work experience and employment partnerships. In the USA the individualistic work ethic and minimal welfare benefits have encouraged more focus on guidance and training for all young people for specific jobs, even if low skill and low level.

Participants' views in New York

The research for this book attempted to combine inquiry into how schools, colleges and administrators described lower attainers, especially those already classed as learning disabled, with views on their likely future in the labour market. As in the UK, participants in the USA were asked who their lower attainers were, what sort of education they were offered and what their futures would be like, and as in all the countries studied the information can only be regarded as a selective snapshot of a range of views. New York has the largest public education system in the USA, with a million students in some 1200 schools. Around 15 per cent of students are regarded as being in need of special education services, the majority being learning disabled, although proportions vary from school to school. For example the Opportunities Charter school in Harlem has over 50 per cent of students classed as LD, with 120 staff serving 400 students and mixed parental views of services (Christ 2010).[4] In addition to payments for special education in the public schools, the city also pays some $824 million out for special needs services in private schools (Ginsberg and Rapp 2010). The city also has its share of voluntary and community associations and organisations often headed by charismatic personnel, aiming to educate lower attaining and disengaged students, and their assumed disorganised families.[5]

The Head of Learning Disability Studies at one of the 26 colleges that make up the City University of New York (CUNY) teaches student teachers in the area of disability studies in education and runs a remedial class for LD students coming into the college, described as a 'fifth year' of high school. His view is that there has been a 'colonisation of the world' by theories of deficit, extending now to Asian countries, and the expansion of numbers of lower-attaining students who are classed as LD is partly due to the removal of stigma associated with the category. Minimal brain dysfunctions have now been overtaken by neuroscience claims and brain development issues, which absolves parents from any guilt associated with parenting and provides welcome explanations for difficult behaviour. Middle-class white parents especially, use mandated city services to have their children 'diagnosed' as LD or having an autistic spectrum disorder, and the city pays for private psychological assessment and expensive private school fees, although the largest group of lower attaining and LD students are still black and Hispanic. At 14/15 all students with an IEP are expected to be given a Transition Plan by the City Department of Education, but in fact some 75 per cent do not get this and only around 25 per cent achieve a regular high school diploma. Most fail to achieve the New York Regent Exam and all many students achieve is an IEP Diploma (Certificate of Attendance). There is general agreement that (following Moxley and Finch 2003) minority LD students are being prepared for the five Fs – low-paid, low-wage and often undesirable jobs.

- Food – fast food outlets, cafes, restaurant workers.
- Filth – cleaning in streets, hotels, offices.
- Folding – laundry work.
- Fetching – messenger work.
- Filing – low-level office work.

He noted that there was a general reluctance to talk about vocational education, although technical and trade schools may be 'making a comeback' and city officials are working to remove the stigma still often associated with a qualification in a vocational area. Working class students often cannot afford to stay on at community colleges to gain vocational qualifications and cannot afford the high fees at private colleges. There is also some opposition from unions who want to limit the intake of young people on vocational courses or in apprenticeships. After 21 there are no mandated services to help LD or other disabled students apart from the Federal Vestin programme whereby those in community college courses can apply for help to buy books, computers and pay for counselling services.

The principal of a school in Lower Manhattan runs a popular and over-subscribed school occupying three floors of the building. He is proud of his school and its 'tough love' message, which helps guarantee good behaviour from students. All poor student behaviour is challenged and he brings parents in for discussion with himself and the student, as he thinks parents should take more responsibility for their children's learning and behaviour. The school takes predominantly Hispanic, black and other minority students and the principal himself is from the Dominican Republic. The school prides itself on the numbers of students who take the Regent Exam and go on to college, and attempts to keep low-attaining young people from dropping out or under-achieving. While all the parents wanted their children to go on to college, taking academic courses, and regarded trade and vocational schools as second rate, he did think that vocational courses, for example plumbing or electrical skills, would engage the lower attainers, but also noted the unions' attempt to control numbers learning the trades. The LD students were mainly withdrawn from mainstream classes and taught separately with special teachers. The two dedicated teachers disliked the labels given to students and did their best to give individual attention to all. One student was described as having a beautiful mind at mathematics, but no social skills. The intention was to prepare all the LD students for college, but there was more risk of them dropping out.

A second high school specialising in design and construction was located on the higher floors of a high-rise building with around 380 students, the building houses four schools. There was one student in a wheelchair who was having problems as the lift had broken down and there are few schools in Manhattan that are wheelchair-friendly! Around 70 students had an IEP for learning disability, and the LD specialist teachers regarded an increase in lower-attaining students at the school as the consequence of inclusive policies and special schools closing. The school specialises in co-teaching with several adults in classrooms and no withdrawal of the LD students. The aim of the school was to put all leavers onto a college course, and if that failed onto a course at the small number of trade or technical schools. Some of the students may attend cooperative schools with a half day in school and a half day at a technical or trade college. There was a post-18 trade school on lower floors teaching catering and food technology and some of the lower-attaining students had the option of transferring there. This was one school where the staff noted that some of the regular students objected to learning in classes with LD students, teasing them as being 'mentally retarded'.

Since the majority of schools in Manhattan are attended by black, Hispanic and other minority students, who go on to a variety of college courses, there are no clear racial distinctions within the public schools and undoubtedly many students progressed to higher course levels. In common with the UK however, many white families have always sought if possible to separate their children in suburban, private or faith schools, and in private special schools. A third school visited was a private fee-paying school for low-attaining, LD and disengaged students regarded as having a variety of special needs. Despite being in the urban setting, the school, originally funded after the Second World War by a rich American who had met and admired a famous English Prime Minister reputed to be a low achiever at school, had its own large building with a garden and excellent facilities. The students were almost entirely white and middle class, and the fees were above $30,000 with many parents able to access city funds. The school employed 75 staff for 400 students, which included counsellors, speech therapists, language specialists and practised co-teaching. Classrooms usually had several adults in them, usually at least two for groups of twelve students, and the Head of Professional Development had many years teaching experience and also trained student teachers at university level. Parental expectations were that their children would go on to a four-year college course and would certainly not be in training for the five F's described above.

Participants' views in Los Angeles schools

Los Angeles, the largest city in California, has a population of some 3.9 million, of whom 35 per cent are under 18. The ethnic breakdown in 2006 was 46.6 per cent classed as white, 11.2 per cent black, 46.5 per cent Hispanic and 10 per cent Asian, with smaller percentages of other groups. (People can identify as 'more than one race'.) In some 58 per cent of homes a language other than English is spoken at home, and 22.1 per cent of people were living below the poverty line. Despite its size and wealth, California does not have a good reputation for public education. In state comparisons, in 2010 Californian 14-year-olds were graded as 46th out of 51 states in maths testing, with one philanthropic 'reformer' blaming elected school boards made up of 'wannabees and unions' for educational failure (*The Economist* 2010b). The California Teachers Association had defeated moves to a school voucher system for school choice, changing probationary period for teachers and linking student progress to teacher job security. Initially the teacher unions opposed the Obama Administration Federal funds for the 'Race to the Top' programme, but eventually capitulated to acquire the extra money. Teachers and unions regard the intense focus on testing and assessment from the No Child Left Behind legislation in much the same way that teachers regard the focus on testing regimes in England and the 'blaming' of schools and teachers for student failure.

Los Angeles Unified District (LAUD) is the largest district in the state and in 2009 there were some 680,000 students in the district, with some 33,500 teachers. The ethnic breakdown in the public schools was 73.1 per cent Hispanic, 10.9 per cent black, 8.7 per cent white, 3.7 per cent Asian, 2.3 per cent Filipino, 4 per cent Pacific islander and 0.3 per cent Alaskan Native. Thus in a city that incorporates nearly 47 per cent of white people only 8.7 per cent are attending public schools. White students are predominantly to be found in private schools, charter schools and faith, especially Catholic schools. Students are expected to gain a high school diploma which entails passing the California High School Exit examination, and credits can be earned in a variety of ways. Some schools offer career technical education classes as a preparation for post-secondary technical and vocational courses and the State has a model of 15 industry sectors and the career pathways for these. For example, in the building and construction sector, careers listed are cabinet making and wood products, engineering and heavy construction, mechanical and commercial construction. In marketing and sales careers listed are e-commerce, entrepreneurship, international trade, and professional and sales marketing (California Career Technical Education Model 2006). Students at school can take paid work from 14, providing they have a work permit, and from 14–15 students can work up to three hours per day and up to eight hours on non-school days. Those with an IEP can have work experience organised for them and the school hands out a pay cheque for this. All students are expected to aim for college courses and the nine campuses of the LA Community College district offers hundreds of courses, both two- and four-year.

The vocational courses typically include agriculture, auto and truck technology, business, computing and office technology, construction and maintenance, communications and marketing, design and visual arts, education and human services, health and science, hospitality, law enforcement and legal services, public administration and sports programmes. For those not attending college, there are Occupational Centres where students can be admitted from 16 in agreement with their school counsellor. The courses at these centres are 'competence-based' in, for example, air conditioning and refrigeration, solar panels, nursing assistant, skin care and manicurist, and all students are expected to take reading and maths courses. The course preparing school janitors included instructions for how to clean and wash walls. The requirement for school janitors to have a qualification is an example of the need for a credential in a job where previously it was not needed.

The Division of Special Education occupies several floors of the large education building in downtown LA although as in the UK, special services, their location and funding, are under review. The Director of Special Services and her team, which included the Directors of Transition, Behavioral Services, and Secondary Instruction, were all knowledgeable about the issues and problems surrounding special education and its expansion. Some 80,000 students, around 12 per cent in the district, were assessed as having special educational needs and had an IEP, and the Division also cares for groups classed as delinquent, at-risk, homeless and teenage pregnancies. The Unified District spends around $1.3 million each year on special education services and much of this money goes on litigation instigated by parents and defending decisions and placements. They noted with some amusement that 'autism in W district nearly bankrupted us'. From 14 all students with an IEP have access to the Transition Service and all high schools have transition teachers who plan the school and after-school careers of the young people, arranging courses and work experience. The District Office of Transition Services (DOTS) noted that 'Transition from school to adult life is a process and we collaborate with families, school personnel, employers and outside agencies, empowering students to make decisions, set goals and carry out their transition plans from school to post-school opportunities'. The office oversees the school services and teachers, and even provided advice to students on how to handle their cheques for work experience. Since schools now include a range of students who were previously excluded there has been an increase in demand for services and funding especially in the moderate/severe range of learning disability, and the DOTS now works with the California Department of Rehabilitation, which offers help to all those 'with a physical or mental impairment' to gain vocational training and employment. This department provides students with an Individualised Plan for Employment (IPE) – not to be confused with an IEP! The staff noted that the District had finally applied for Federal money under the 'Race to the Top' programme, but thought that as 'there is no let-up in testing and assessment' this was yet another 'punitive strategy on schools and teachers'.

The Head of Transition Services in a large high school in the north of the District currently deals with around 250 students with IEPs out of a school population of 2000. The school has a broad curriculum, which includes Latin and is set in a tree-lined campus with two magnet centres for performing arts and medical services, a working auto-machine shop servicing cars, wood, carpentry and metal-working shops, IT rooms, and a military cadet building. All males have to register for military service at 18 but are not drafted unless war demands it, and the over-representation of black young people in the military has led to claims that this is another way of marginalising them. The Head of Transition was meeting with three students aged 15, 17 and 18, doing their work experience in childcare, medical assistance and chef work, respectively. They had come to collect their cheques, which as with the EMA in England, was a help with their expenses and a stimulus to completing courses. They felt 'it was like doing real work to get a wage' and were certainly acquiring the idea that work brings money. These students, and others with an IEP who do not go on to college will go on to the local Occupational Centre for further courses in their chosen areas. The aim of the Head of Transition was to get all students with IEPs onto college or Centre courses with no drop outs.

At a large high school in central LA with some 2,500 students and set in a campus area with several buildings, including one for students with disabilities, the teachers were clear that although the school was inclusive, there was a difference between mild LD, where 'students were simply lower attainers' and moderate to severe LD. The school population was 54 per cent Hispanic, 19 per cent Asian, 17 per cent black, 3 per cent Filipino and 7 per cent white and the LD students were from all backgrounds. From 14 the LD students were told about transition and given folders to work with, learning how to write CVs and discussing possible college courses and jobs. In class students were encouraged to discuss their futures and to question visitors (including myself) on their education and careers. In these classes, if any deaf or hearing-impaired students are present, the state requires a signer to be present. In one class the students had ambitions which included chef, music technology and care jobs. In a separate class for moderate LD, there were four staff to twenty students, several of whom were in wheelchairs with helpers and these students were also learning about college and jobs. The teachers thought there had been an increase in those with moderate LD and were more likely to refer these students to the regional rehabilitation centres after school.

At a nearby high school with a pleasant campus, the head was in charge of some 2,500 students, of whom 62 per cent were Hispanic, 17 per cent black (and mainly bussed in from another area of town), 9 per cent Asian, 2 per cent Filipino and 9 per cent white. The transition team noted that there had been a large increase in those labelled as having autistic spectrum disorders, but were sceptical of the claims made by families, supported by psychologist and medical personnel, that their children and in some cases whole families, suffered from the disorders. They noted the willingness of parents to go to law to claim their 'right' to special educational services, and this was one school that had overspent on litigation and these services. The view was that many parents were 'helicopter parents', hovering over their children to protect them from failure on high-level courses and in job competition. There was also an increase in elementary school teachers claiming that children had autistic disorders or aggressive-compulsive disorders, and much medication, usually Ritalin, was given out for this. This school also had a class for moderate LD students, overseen by a cheerful teacher wearing a pink pinafore. She taught basic skills, computer use, cooking and laundry with the aim of independent living for the students if they did not make it onto lower-level college courses.

At a high school in a 'whiter' suburb, the school was 75 per cent black, the students being bussed in, 15 per cent Hispanic, 8 per cent white and 2 per cent Asian. The campus was large and tidy and the head noted that students volunteered at weekends to come in to pick up litter and paint the school – a contrast to the English students noted in Chapter 4 who thought picking up litter 'beneath them'. The LD teacher took 8–10 students in her small room, her view being that this helped concentration and writing. At 17–19 the students spent time practising writing college applications, writing CVs and learning about jobs. They were told that all students need a Social Security Number to apply for community college and that they would have priority for popular courses. They were also told they would have to pay for courses but could get fee assistance from several sources, including the Department for Rehabilitation. The Department looks for lower cost programmes and will pay if the student works and remains in the programme. They were also told about adult trade schools and Occupational Centre courses and that some centres provide food and accommodation, courses such as auto-mechanics, construction, vet and pharma assistant were mentioned. Later some of the students were observed on work experience at a nearby university. Several boys were learning to service machinery, although one said he wanted to join the marines, one girl was helping in the post room and another in the media department. One student, on being introduced to the visitor, announced that 'he had never met a European before'!

A large (22,000) community college in the District was visited where a centre for students with moderate LD was housed in a Portakabin™. The students on this programme were mainly Hispanic and several had physical and sensory disabilities. They were all on low-level courses, learning basic skills and doing work experience which was heavily supervised. The teachers stressed that many of the students lacked social skills and an understanding of living independently. Many had never travelled on buses and time was spent taking them on buses and teaching other skills for independent living. There was little contact between these students and those on regular college courses, and the view was that they were unlikely to find work after college.

Conclusions

The aim of this chapter was to provide some comparative information with England as to who were described as lower attainers or in need of special education in schools and colleges after age 14, what sort of education and training is offered to them and what future envisaged for them. Although education systems differ between countries in terms of their history, values and practices, there are many similarities between the two countries in how they deal with their lower attainers. This is partly due to the global ideology and accompanying rhetoric that education systems must now incorporate all groups and individuals formerly excluded, and train or give them credentials so that they can function in national economies, albeit at lower levels. In both countries it is no longer acceptable for even low-level jobs to be filled by the untrained and uncredentialled, and school and college courses have expanded in both countries to deal with the situation. School and college personnel now take for granted that exclusion from training, work and social development is no longer acceptable and in both countries work experience of some kind is also a necessity. There is however a difference in attitudes to work and practices, in the USA the individualist work ethic and minimal welfare state benefits encourage more focus on informing and training young people for specific jobs, albeit low level. In the UK, although young people want work, government prefers to stress the penalties for not working. In the USA special education is what Brantlinger has described as a 'highly legalised tracking system' (Brantlinger 2008: 238). In both countries the expansion of special education and dealing with lower attainers is now a crucial part of mass education systems in a global economy, preparing lower-class young people for lower-level jobs, and acting as a palliative strategy for middle-class parents who are often desperate to keep their young in more privileged circumstances. In both countries there is no evidence that middle-class parents are enthusiastic for their children to take vocational courses or manual jobs.

There is undoubtedly evidence that in both countries fear of losing out in the competitive educational and employment conditions that market societies have created, parents have become more demanding of resources that would give their children what are perceived as improved chances for success, or provide explanations for their failure. The demand for special educational services and resources is an inevitable consequence of policies to 'raise standards' and pressure schools and teachers into credentialing more children at ever higher levels. If the raising standards agenda has led schools and teachers into strategies of teaching to tests, narrowing the curriculum, dishonest reporting and litigation over funding, it has also led to parental distrust of schools and teachers, with parents encouraged to be critics and vigilantes rather than partners in their children's education. In the expansion of demand for special educational services in mainstream, special classes and the remaining segregated schooling, the expansion of professional vested interest, especially in medical, psychological and therapeutic interests, continues to be served, and this expansion is enormously expensive in both countries. Race and class are powerful tools for understanding the way educational opportunities are distributed both in the USA and the UK and in both countries antagonisms are the product of history, and current economic and social contexts. In England lower attainers are predominantly part of the disadvantaged urban and some rural poor, with attention focused on these white students, and those of African Caribbean heritage, other selected minority groups and refugees. In the USA the lower attainers and the 'special' still come predominantly from African American and Hispanic groups, educational chances exacerbated by spatial racial segregation. As is increasingly demonstrated in both the USA and Europe, the continued global economic crisis and competition for jobs is likely to increase racial antagonisms in claims for educational resources and privileges.

Notes

1 This quote suggests that the writer had previously been in the naval services, possibly a stoker! It was the case in England for many years that schools for the severely intellectually- and physically-disabled employed untrained ex-marines and other service people.

2 Among other organisations the National Centre for Educational Statistics (NCES) which collects data for the Federal Government on all aspects of education, reports regularly that black and Hispanic students are more likely than whites to drop out of high school before obtaining a diploma, as are students with a disability or who are lower achievers (see Chapman, Laird, Ramani 2011).

3 An example of this would be the 'Response to Intervention' (RTI) programme developed to help teachers assess student difficulties and help them via three stages. A debate ensued as to whether the method was to be used by special education teachers as well as in general classrooms (Fuchs, Fuchs, Compton 2011).

4 Charter schools, first introduced in Minnesota in 1991, have the same contentious history as academy schools in England, with State Public Education Boards and Commissions, teachers, unions and parents divided over their introduction and funding arrangements. The schools receive public money but have more autonomy and fewer constraints on hiring staff, curriculum requirements and so on. A study in 2009 by the Centre for Research in Educational Outcomes at Stanford University found that of all the charter schools studied, 17 per cent had better test results than other public schools, 40 per cent similar results and 37 per cent worse results.

5 An example of this is the Harlem Children's Zone Inc., a non-profit-making agency which runs projects and programmes for children and adults in Harlem. The president and CEO is Geoffry Canada, later offered the post of City Chancellor of New York Schools by the Mayor, and President Obama suggested extending the model into other cities.

Appendix 1 Special education classification, United States, 1920–2005

	1920s	1950s	1960s	1970s	2005
SOCIAL	Speech defectives	Speech defectives	Speech problems	Speech & language impairments	Speech/language impairments
	Incorrigibles	Delinquent	Emotionally disturbed	Serious emotional disturbance	Emotionally disturbed
	Socially maladjusted		Socially maladjusted		
INTELLECTUAL	Most highly endowed	Specially-gifted	Gifted	Gifted & talented	Gifted & talented
	Dullest of the normal group	Gifted		Learning disabilities	Specific learning disabilities
	Backward Imbecile Idiot (...)	Feeble-minded	Trainable mentally-retarded	Mental retardation	Mental retardation
			Educable mentally-retarded		Developmental delay (1997–)
					Autism (1992–)
SENSORY	Blind	Blind	Blind	Visually handicapped	Visual impairments
		Defective vision	Partially seeing	Deaf-blind (1979–)	Deaf-blindness
	Deaf	Deaf	Deaf	Deaf	Hearing impairments
		Defective hearing	Partially hearing	Hard of hearing	
PHYSICAL	Crippled	Crippled	Crippled	Orthopedically impaired	Orthopedic impairments
		Delicate	Chronic health cases	Other health impaired	Other health impairments
				Multiply handicapped (1979–)	Multiple disabilities
					Traumatic brain injury (1992–)
	The Education of Exceptional Children (Horn 1924)	*The Education of Exceptional Children* (Heck 1953)	*Exceptional Children in the Schools* (Dunn 1963)	*Education for All Handicapped Children Act* (1975) *Gifted and Talented Children's Education Act* (1978)	*Individuals with Disabilities Education Act* (*Annual Report to Congress*)

Source: adapted from J.W. Powell 'Change in disability classification: redrawing categorical boundaries in special education in the United States and Germany 1920–2005', *Comparative Sociology*, 9:241–267.

Chapter 6

Germany

Transition to where?

> The German economy is currently playing in a league of its own.
>
> (Kollewe 2010)

Germany has the largest national economy in Europe, is the world's second-largest exporter, and 37 of the top 500 stock market listed companies have their headquarters in the country.

In the world economic crisis since 2008 the German economy continued to function well, although changes to the labour market suggested by the Hartz Committee (Hartz 2010 and see below) were intended to help with unemployment. In the 'eurozone crisis'[1] which subsequently affected most European Union countries, Germany played a leading role in attempting to stabilise other economies. Much of this performance is credited to a strong manufacturing sector which in turn benefits from the high levels of skill of the workforce, trained in the dual system of apprenticeships in all industrial and commercial sectors, and where, until recently, it was possible for vocational training to be offered to a majority of young people. While there is less rhetoric about a 'knowledge economy' than in other countries, it is taken for granted that the economy needs a highly qualified labour force at all levels. English admiration for German education and training has a long history. Writing in *The Times* newspaper in 1916, Sir Michael Sadler, Master of University College Oxford, wrote, with some academic and class snobbery, that 'German education makes good use of all second grade ability which in England is far too much of a waste product . . . it has not made profitable use of second grade intelligence' (Sadler 1916). While Sadler perpetuated the notion that education which was not academic was for those with lower abilities, he misunderstood the respect which was given to the *Beruf* – the trade or occupation which defined German vocational training and which included the notion of the full development of each young person (Idriss 2002). But as in other countries, there are increasing numbers of lower-attaining young people, who while obliged to stay in education and training until 18, cannot find a place in the dual system and are candidates for what is described as a transition system, 'an unwanted and neglected part of VET – vocational and education training provision' (Ertl 2009). These young people plus those who leave from the segregated special education sector are likely candidates for unemployment. This chapter discusses the German selective education system, including the segregated special education sector, vocational education and its changes, and reports the views of some college and school staff on arrangements for lower attainers.

Education and selection

Like the USA, Germany illustrates a decentralised system, in which 16 Lander (states), five of them former East German (GDR) states, function independently but under the wider jurisdiction of the Federal Government. Education is the responsibility of each Land, but legislation and guidance from the Federal Government must be adhered to, and there is a conference of the 16 Lander ministers (Kultusministerkonferenz) who coordinate the policies of the states. In Germany, as in England, secondary education developed during the nineteenth century within a clear social and selective hierarchy. The Gymnasium, with its classical curriculum, was the school for the upper and professional classes, the Realschule and Oberrealschule offered industrial and scientific education to the commercial classes, and early trade schools – Gewerbeschulen – developed from the 1820s, taught specific trades. Green (1990) pointed out that the Realschule and trade schools were actually attended by larger numbers of students than attended the Gymnasium, but they were predominantly from the lower class and artisan families. Although the education system remains largely selective from aged ten, after four years of primary school, and the Gymnasium is still the most sought after school, there was early on good schooling for young people in technical and industrial skills, even if regarded as 'second-grade ability'. During the twentieth century especially in post-Second World War reconstruction the 'Beruf' became the defining element in the German vocational system, in which a majority of young people were prepared for a future occupation. The dual system of part-time work and part-time schooling after 16, which involved collaboration between employers, colleges and government, was regarded as a central element in German industrial reconstruction and a subsequent strong economy. It was also regarded as a broad way of preparing young people for their social democracy.

In explaining the persistence of selective schooling in Germany, Ertl and Phillips (2000) noted the way in which the five Lander of the former GDR opted to adopt the West German model of selective secondary schooling rather than stay with the East German model of a comprehensive schooling. In this all children stayed together from 6–16 in the Einheitsschule, leading on for the majority to vocational Berufsschule, in which 'There was a basic principle that everybody is eligible for training and have some certainty about their future working life. That includes the handicapped and disadvantaged students' (Neather 2000: 25). With some differences between states the model remains:

- Gymnasium (grammar school) intended for 'theoretically-inclined students', prepared for university via the Abitur at 18/19. The course of study at this type of school was recently shortened from nine years to eight, with some parental protest.
- Realschule (intermediate school) preparing students who will go on to technical and higher skilled vocational training, with a final leaving certificate, the Realschulabschluss.
- Hauptschule (secondary school) offering a basic general education for students with 'practical talents' leading on to vocational training, with a final leaving certificate, the Hauptschulabschuluss, at 16. In some south German states Hauptschule is only nine years, while in others, for example North Rhine-Westphalia, it is ten years and students can also leave with a certificate equivalent to the Realschule certificate.
- Gesamtschule (comprehensive school) offers the three types of education described above but in one institution.

As Ertl and Phillips (2000) pointed out, few countries retain such early selection and the German system has been subject to international criticism. The major defence is that the system operates on the basis of 'parental choice', albeit heavily guided by teachers and transfer reports. The first year at secondary school is an orientation year after which students can move school, but few move away from the Gymnasium, attended in all Lander by some 33 per cent of students and with only around 11 per cent of working-class children attending. The popularity of the Realschule has been attributed to the high standards of pre-vocational education and training, which prepares students for entry into the dual system and then into commercial, technical and administrative fields. It is also possible to move from Realschule to the Gymnasium and take the Abitur. The Hauptschule is less popular and is attended largely by working-class students and 'foreigners', mainly Turkish and Kurdish children, many of whose parents do not have German citizenship. Despite being born in Germany and with German as a first language, many of these young people are regarded as 'Migrationshintergrund',[2] and are disadvantaged in education and training. They have always been over-represented in the Hauptschule, are more likely to be thought to be in need of special education, less likely to find places in the dual system (even with good educational achievements), and have been blamed for bringing down the German scores in the international PISA comparisons (Mannitz 2004). The unequal incorporation of minorities into European education systems continues to be a political issue in Germany, as elsewhere (Luchtenberg 2005, Tomlinson 2010b). In a special report to the United Nations Human Rights Council, Munoz (2007) urged the German Government to consider changes to the multi-tier school system which does lead to discrimination against working class and minority students. He also noted the separation of children with physical or intellectual disabilities from mainstream schools and urged a rights-based approach to changing this.

Some states have begun to change the composition of their school systems, merging the Hauptschule and Realschule, or introducing Gesamtschule alongside other schools. In North Rhine-Westphalia Gesamtschulen were introduced from the 1970s under the Social Democrat Government, and there are currently some 204 Gesamtschulen to 518 Gymnasia. More recently the Social Democrat and Green parties in the state support a 'Gemeinschaftsschule' or community school which could be combined with a primary school. Other states remain relentlessly selective from age ten. In Bavaria for example, there are no Gesamtschulen, and in Hamburg in 2010 a parental vote was to keep early selection, due to 'a furious middle class reaction' against a more egalitarian proposal (*The Economist* 2010b). Indeed, a backlash against proposed school reform forced the Hamburg Mayor, a Christian Democrat, to resign his position, even though evidence was clear that school selection discriminated against lower class and migrant children (Topping 2011). A major issue with the German education system is that it mainly functions on half-day schedules, and it is usually mothers who are expected to collect the children. Women who want to work full-time are thus disadvantaged, especially working-class women who cannot easily take time off. The issue has recently been the focus of debate and change (see Hagermann, Jarausch, Allemann-Ghionda 2010) and some schools are moving to an all-day model. Teachers in German schools, as in Finland, are expected to operate as pedagogic professionals with a minimum of five years training, which includes child development, psychology and educational theory. Most schools employ social workers with a diploma in social pedagogy and there is little expectation that teachers will engage in 'raising self-esteem' or exploring identities, other than in their subject lessons, although, as Luchtenberg has pointed out, Germany still lacks the concept of itself as composed of diverse groups and cultures (Luchtenberg 2005: 14).

Special schooling

Most discussion of selective education in Germany ignores the selection of children out of the system of mainstream schooling into special schooling and thus into a limited future in terms of vocational education and future life chances. Some 6 per cent of young people are withdrawn at early stages from mainstream education and according to the Standing Conference of Ministers of Education and Culture 'attend special forms of general education and vocational school types – partly integrated with non-handicapped pupils depending on the disability in question' (SCMEC 2009). In fact, once assessed and placed in special school – formerly Sonderschule, now referred to as Forderschule – support school, it is very difficult for students to return to mainstream schools or vocational training. Although Germany ratified the 2006 UN Convention of the Rights of Persons with Disabilities which required inclusive education, German segregated special education has continued to expand. Pfahl and Powell (2011: 450) note that 'While many countries [*sic*] education systems have become more inclusive,

Germany's remains overwhelmingly segregative'. Powell (2010), analysing the special education categories that developed during the twentieth century, noted that these are similar in complexity and subject to the same arbitrary changes as those in England or the USA, and also subject to similar stigma. As in other countries, early categorisations were heavily influenced by eugenic ideologies concerning the disabled and handicapped; Germany in the Nazi era instigating a forced regime of sterilization and euthanasia for the 'mentally and physically handicapped', and classification was always dependent on medical and individual deficit models. In 1954 the Federal Statistics Office classified children by school type into ten, then in 1994, nine categories:

- Learning disability (Lernen).
- Emotional and social development (Emotionale und sociale Entwicklung).
- Mental development (Gestige Entwicklung).
- Bodily and motor development (Korperliche und motorische Entwicklung).
- Health patients (Kranke).
- Speech (Sprache).
- Sight (Sehen).
- Hearing (Horen).
- Multiple and unclassified (Mehrfach/nicht Klassifizert) (see Powell 2011: 261).

The designation 'Kruppelschulen' – Cripples School – was only changed to school for the physically disabled in 1964. It is the category of learning disability – Lernbehinderung – which as elsewhere, has become the largest category of special educational support, and as elsewhere it is the children of the lower socio-economic groups and minorities that overwhelmingly fall into this category. Having a learning difficulty is mainly the prerogative of the socially disadvanted and minorities, Turkish and Kurdish children in particular, being over-represented in special schools (Kormann 2003). As elsewhere, assessment for special schools is heavily dependent on psychological testing and assessment, and 'diagnosis' of dyslexia and attention deficit syndrome began to appear in the 1980s, requiring special schooling, the latter in schools for social and emotional problems. There is more stress on paternalistic notions of separate 'educational support' than other countries, and there is no category for the 'gifted and talented'. A major reason for the resistance to inclusive education is the German special education profession, who together with their union representation, well-paid jobs and status, have strong vested interests in segregation. An Association of Support Schools, founded in 1898, later became a Professional Association for the Disabled, finally settling in 2003 on Verband Deutscher Sonderpadagogik – Association of German Special Education. The professional associations have been 'highly influential in constructing differences and maintaining a classification system that underpins separate special schools' (Pfahl and Powell 2011–460). The majority of students leave the special education sector without a school-leaving certificate and are counted in official statistics as school drop outs. The Federal Standing Conference of Ministers of Education and Cultural Affairs are currently discussing the development of a Sonderschule Certificate, which would make it easier for special school leavers to move on to vocational programmes and help the drop out statistics.

Vocational education and training

There is a large and long-standing literature on German vocational education and the dual system, both admiring and critical, and its relationship to the labour market (Taylor 1981, Witte and Kallenberg 1995), and comparisons with other countries are frequently made. As Green and Steedman pointed out, 'Education and training contributes to the skills which enable countries to compete in international markets, and governments increasingly assess the adequacy of the skill levels in their own population in relation to those of key competitors' (Green and Steedman 1997: 1). In Germany the states have control over their own education systems, including vocational schools and colleges, but the Federal Government regulates apprenticeship training outside schools, in industry, firms, shops, offices hotels and so on. There are around 350 state-regulated occupations making up every aspect of economic life, with some 45 per cent of all young people from 16 and above being in the dual system at any time, the majority in part-time work, part-time college, but some in full-time college-based training. By the 1990s the dual system of training for one occupation came in for criticism as changes in the economy brought new jobs, and there was a growing reluctance of some employers to participate (Ertl 2004, Kupfer 2010). While talk of a crisis in the dual system has previously occurred during recessions, the problems in vocational training in the 2000s were largely the result of a changing economy. Although there was no simple rhetoric of a 'knowledge economy', with jobs in industry and manufacturing remaining important, requirements for new technologies and communications became more obvious. Munoz (2007: 13) wrote that as in all OECD countries, globalisation increases the need for highly qualified workers, unskilled workers are less likely to be needed and low attainers who do not acquire access to further education are likely to be excluded from the economy. Kupfer (2010) criticised the dual system for selecting young women for traditional female apprenticeships, in hairdressing and as medical assistants for example, but in the technical areas, women are now sought as male applications decline, although competition for places in information technology is fierce. Women are encouraged to participate in new sectors in the economy, but as noted, employers usually view women as the primary parent once children come along and are less willing to employ or promote them. In addition, the effects of participating in a European Union in which workers can move around between countries has affected the employment of young Germans. A committee chaired initially by the Personnel Director of Volkswagen set in train some reforms to the lower market (Hartz 2010: 1–1V), which included more Federal support for vocational education and the introduction of mini and midi jobs, by which employees would pay lower taxes for shorter hours (Hartz 2010).

The dual system is currently the subject of research and debate and one project, comparing vocational education and training in Germany and England, summarised problems facing the system as:

- A shortage of skilled labour overall.
- Demographic changes affecting fluctuating demand for places.
- Variations between sectors with a surplus in some areas and insufficient places in others.
- Some sectors with no dual system tradition, e.g. information technology.
- University first degrees in competition for higher levels in the dual system.
- An increasing number of young people deemed unsuitable for the dual system (see Higham, Kremer, Yeomans 2009).

It is this last group which is of interest here, as the students noted are predominantly the lower attainers in school, many leaving without having obtained the lowest school-leaving certificate (the Hauptschulabschulss). Although some states have begun to experiment with vocational special schools, there are few records of what these are offering and limited research on the destinations of the special school leavers. While there have been a variety of Federal and state responses to the decline of some sectors in the dual system, most states have developed a 'transition sector' which overall currently incorporates students who cannot find a place in the dual system or any kind of employment. Those who drop out of education and training completely or work in the 'black economy' would increase the official numbers. Higham, Kremer, Yeomans (2009) have described provision in the transition sector as:

- Students taking a basic one-year vocational training (Berufgrundschuljahr) which can be accepted as equivalent to the first year in the dual system.
- A pre-vocational year (Beruforientierungsjahr) which gives some experience of different occupations.
- Courses for students without apprenticeships (Klassen fur Schueler/innen ohne Beruf) with two days in vocational college and three work experience with an employer or provided by the Labour Office.
- Full-time training leading to a certificate (Hoehere Berufsfacschule). This can include occupations such as kindergarten teacher, who are not required to have a degree.

While a transition sector incorporating these various school/college-based programmes may keep young people in education and training and some may progress to higher-level programmes or into the dual system, many of the transition programmes, as in some English colleges, attempt to keep young people on courses with little possibility of progression. Ertl (2009) suggested that the transition system is neglected by policy makers, who appear to regard it as a temporary issue, but as fewer than a third of those on the transition courses go on into the dual system or full-time training, transition into the labour market is problematic. 'Transition to where?' may be a realistic question for many young people. Kupfer has suggested that as those with higher-level school-leaving certificates take a decreasing number of apprenticeships, those with lower-level or no certificates lose out, and 'as a short-term reaction, middle class students are replacing the working class in vocational education' (Kupfer 2010: 93). As elsewhere, the middle classes in Germany are struggling to defend their children's position in a problematic world, and more social inequality is one consequence of changes in vocational training.

Participants' views

To help understand what is happening to lower attainers in schools and colleges, especially those who leave with no certificate, a Berufskolleg, a Hauptschule and three Gesamtschulen in one large city in the state of North Rhine-Westphalia were visited. As in visits in other countries, information can only be regarded as a snapshot of views. Colleagues at the university in that city however, were particularly interested in the relationship between education and the labour market and their work is referred to in the final chapter of this book.

North Rhine-Westphalia (NRW) is Germany's most heavily populated state with some 18 million people, and covers the industrial Ruhr area as well as large agricultural areas. It is an economically-productive state, accounting for some 22 per cent of German GDP, although unemployment at 9.5 per cent in 2009 (down to 8.1 per cent in 2010), was above the average for Germany. There are currently over 2.1 million young people attending schools from primary to the end of secondary school. As in other states, a decline in the number of apprentice-ships available and the question of what to do with lower-attaining young people, mainly from the working class, minority and migrant groups looms large and has led to a number of projects, many under a Federal Programme of Youth and Work (Jugend und Beruf). For example, an 'Experiment in third way apprenticeships', set up in 2006 and funded by the European Social Fund, targeted young people with no school-leaving certificate and prepared them for apprenticeships over five years (Bosel 2008). Students were prepared in three 'blocks', at an educational institution, a vocational school and a workplace or enterprise in 14 types of occu-pation. These included warehouse worker, mechanic, hotel and catering, furni-ture, kitchen, tailoring, removal services, engines and metal work, building and construction, chemical sector, driving and underground worker.

The director and staff at a large Berufskolleg for craft and technical studies (Handwerk und Tecknik) confirmed the national picture, as in this college there were around 43.5 per cent of young people in the dual system, 16 per cent of these on college-based-only apprenticeships, with some 39.7 per cent of students not in apprenticeships and in the transition system. Around 70 per cent of students at this college were male and gender separation was evident, with girls more likely to be in hairdressing and food technology courses, boys in carpentry, construction and electrical courses. Students attending the college could progress from entry at 16 to university or higher technical training (Fachhofschule). The lower-attaining students were those who came from the Hauptschule either with a certificate but had not actually completed a final year there, or those who came without a certificate, including a few from special schools. Those with a certificate went onto the one-year vocational course which could lead to an apprenticeship or the one-year vocational course which could lead to progression to higher-level courses. Those without certificates went on the work orientation year which might then lead to the pre-vocational course. The college also ran courses in association with the Youth and Work Programme, paid for by the Labour Office. The students on these courses were described as 'the lower 30 per cent, often from problem families into alcohol and crime'. While the aim of all the lower-level courses was to give some kind of education and training, the college director and staff were all of the opinion that the expansion of courses was 'a reaction to the lack of jobs, the labour market is the crucial factor, no-one knows how to manage wage problems in the global economy'. The Job Centres (Labour Offices) fund students 16–25 but there are not enough jobs at the end. One lecturer noted that he had worked in many different training institutions and

> there was a time when highly skilled craftsmen found employment. Employers were convinced this was the best way. Now employers say it costs too much to take on apprentices as the job preparation will not be financed. So what happens? Some firms employ young people as apprentices in jobs they can't do so many drop out, skip vocational school and finally stop preparing for a job. They will find it difficult to get work later on and few social welfare institutions will help.

He also noted that even the hard-working students on the lower-level courses were a problem as they liked the practical work but disliked the reading and writing in classrooms, and many had problems with literacy. As in other countries and states, in this college the young people on the lower-level courses were from working/non-working class/minority backgrounds, and they were the ones most likely to drop out and remain unemployed. There were however, comments from a number of school and college staff that young people were refusing apprenticeships in some areas, with bakers for example, as 'they do not like getting up early'!

The Hauptschule visited was in a part of the city settled by immigrant minorities. The 300 students aged 10–16 at the school came from 30 countries, the majority Turkish, Kurdish Iraqi and some Iranian students, all mostly Muslim. The principal noted that there is a clear social class divide in schooling in the city, the Gymnasia take around 40 per cent of mainly white middle-class students, the nine Hauptschulen take mainly working class and minorities. The level of poverty in the school can be demonstrated by the fact that some 70 per cent of students receive help in paying for their textbooks, as all parents are expected to do. The school works hard to try to integrate students and in the first two years there is a family programme to bring families together; Turkish is taught as a 'mother-tongue' and part of the curriculum is in Turkish. However, he noted that the four years of primary school were too short for migrant and minority children to 'catch up' and it was unsurprising that most came in to the Hauptschule and then went on to lower-level courses in college. He thought the area was becoming more encapsulated, as young people watch Turkish TV, work in local restaurants and seldom leave the area. He also thought that many employers still discriminated against Turkish students. Most of the parents of his students would like their children to go to comprehensive schools, but there were too few in the city. Nevertheless his staff worked hard to give all the students the leaving certificate and the school was helped by a scheme called *Tabula*, in which retired teachers volunteered to teach a variety of activities in and out of school. Although regarded as some of the lower attainers in the whole school system, the students themselves referred to their classmates with more obvious learning difficulties as 'dumbkinder'.[3]

By 2010 there were four comprehensive schools in the city, one in a southern suburb was established in 1997 and fully staffed to teach up to the Abitur by 2005. The students mainly study together until 16 and then move on to either more academic or more vocational courses, after counselling and the production of an individual plan for each student (Individuelle Foederung) which 'takes account of student inclinations and personal development'. Gesamtschule is becoming more popular since the Gymnasium shortened its course from nine to eight years, but parents prefer the longer Gesamtschule courses. This school builds project work both in and outside school into the curriculum for all students with the aim of 'helping students achieve a better understanding of the world they live and work in', and there are links with other schools and with employers for the projects. The principal was clear that project work 'enables students to gain an insight into vocational training and career planning'. One communication project enabled students to work with Internet access and exchange with schools abroad. A major aim of the school is that all students leave familiar with the latest information technology. As a comprehensive school lower attainers are given special attention, but the school is not equipped for physically-disabled students or those with severe-learning difficulties. Counsellors, including student counsellors, 'advise' badly-behaved students and this is one school where staff discuss raising student self-esteem.

A second comprehensive school to the north of the city had adapted to taking students with a range of aptitude, German teachers tending to refer to aptitude (Eignung) rather than 'ability', and the school had won awards for positive support for all students. A detailed description of how the school accommodates all students was described as four 'lighthouses'. The first describes early contact with parents and the information given to them, especially the move at 16 to upper secondary level to different academic or vocational areas, and at 18 to university level, with particular information given on the jobs which need a university education. The second lighthouse describes the remedial language courses given in the first two years for those young people with literacy difficulties, a migrant or second-language background plus courses from years 7–10 (13–16) for those with problems in German, Maths, English and Science. This is also one school where there were advanced courses for the 'very gifted'. The third lighthouse refers to help given to lower attainers in the form of study skills, fewer lessons each day to give more time for learning, co-teaching and cooperative methods in class. The fourth lighthouse notes the variety of clubs and after-school activities, partnerships with other schools including a school in Scotland and partnerships with private companies and other institutions. From year 7 (13–14) students learn about jobs and work orientation, including holding separate 'girl days'. This school also encouraged students to help with cleaning and removing litter.

A third comprehensive school, the first to be opened in the city, was located in an unusual building next to the city university. The school, founded by a well-known German Professor of Education, takes children from 5–18 and is organised on an open-plan model in a long building on several levels. The school quickly became well-known nationally and internationally and is much visited. On the lower levels primary-age children have open classroom areas, including small kitchens for cooking, and on higher levels secondary-age students also mainly work in open-plan areas, with separate rooms for art and design, handicrafts and quiet study. There is a large assembly/theatre, outdoor facilities for sport and movement and much contact with other schools and with the university. The school keeps students of all aptitudes together for much longer than in other schools, gives much information on work, vocational studies and academic courses, but most students stay in the academic track. The school offers help to 'slower learners' and those described as having special needs.

As in most areas of migrant and minority settlement in Germany, the city has a number of projects aimed at integrating young people, offering language and other classes, advising and orienting them to vocational courses and possible work. Turkish and Kurdish young people born in Germany are a target for many projects and around a dozen are brought together in the RAA (Amt fuer Integration und interkutlurelle Angeleghenten) organised from the city town hall and funded partly by the city and partly by the State. Individuals, even those working in other institutions, give time to run the projects and classes, one being a member of staff of the Berefskolleg visited. It is these young people who are most likely to be regarded as lower attainers in the German school system, and as noted, more likely to be in or have left the Hauptschule or special schools without certificates, to be in college transition programmes, to have dropped out of education or training or never to have attended school.

Conclusion

The German education and training system, in contrast to England and the USA, has a long history of attempting to equip all young people, whether regarded as higher or lower attainers, in training programmes that would lead on to some kind of employment. The fit between the education and labour market has thus been much closer than in other countries, and despite the high regard for intellectual knowledge (and the length of time needed to acquire a university degree), even a university education was intended to fit with possible employment. The specific German problem is the partial decline in the dual system, which more or less guaranteed a qualification for a particular occupation and which has led to an expansion of lower-level vocational courses in colleges, as in other countries. What is referred to as the transition system – the various school- and college-based education and training programmes – is now widespread and with a reduction in the number of jobs available for lower attainers and lower-skilled young people, their possibilities in the labour market become problematic. The move by middle-class students, armed with higher-level school certificates, into apprenticeships, further disadvantages the working-class lower attainers. There are similarities with the English system in that colleges are providing a variety of lower-level transition courses which do not have specific aims, other than provide for some kind of certificate that will allow progression to another course, and a proliferation of qualifications and certificates not recognised by employers. The similarities will probably be greater by 2015 when the official school leaving age in England is raised to 18.

The continued segregation of numbers of young people in special schools, and their lack of school-leaving qualifications, is also beginning to be regarded as problematic. Teachers may be resistant to the notion of inclusive education, but on leaving special schools a majority of students with learning difficulties merge with mainstream lower attainers from the Hauptschule in searching for some kind of vocational training and a place in the economy. The German government, as in other countries, aims to make all citizens productive if possible, driven less by rhetoric of a knowledge economy, more by human capital ideologies and the need to reduce welfare dependency. As in all European countries and the USA, statistics continue to record the same pattern of racial, ethnic, migrant and minority young people more likely to be lower attainers either from mainstream or special schools, and to be in lower-level vocational courses with problematic futures. Those working with the young people take it for granted that most of the lower attainers will be from working class and/or minority homes, with issues of poverty, family unemployment and possible futures as drop outs and criminality. More positively than in other countries though, those working with the young people are more likely to make links with a shrinking labour market, low wages and the whole economy rather than regarding the young people and their families as deficient.

Notes

1 A single European currency – the euro – was agreed in 1992 after the Maastricht Treaty created a European Union. It was first introduced in 1999 and became a common currency for most existing EU members in 2002. The global financial crisis of 2008 and a further crisis in 2011 left the eurozone in recession and in 'crisis'. Germany, as the richest EU country, played a large part in stabilising the currency and the Chancellor Angela Merkel was described in one English newspaper as 'the real leader of Europe' (Traynor 2012).

2 Definitions of Migrationshintergrund are: a person who does not have German citizenship, a person born outside German borders of 1949, or with one parent born outside the borders of 1949 (Statistisches Bundesamt Deutschland. Erschienen. 2007).

3 Although this study did not include student views on their own education or classmates, Lisa Pfahl and Justin Powell supplied a list of 46 derogatory names which students in schools in north Germany use to describe their fellow students in special schools or with learning difficulties.

Chapter 7

Malta
Colonial and religious legacies

> Malta cannot be studied . . . as though it were an isolated unit. It is part of
> a wider global society and the influence of the wider global order appears
> almost everywhere.
>
> (Giddens 1994: xxix)

The island of Malta, plus the smaller islands of Gozo and Comino, are located at
a strategic point in the Mediterranean, and function with a centralised education
system heavily influenced by a colonial legacy and by the powerful presence of the
Catholic Church. Although there are much smaller numbers of young people
than in the USA or other European systems, the problems of dealing with lower-
attaining students in a globalising economy are becoming more evident and are
similar to those in other developed countries. The neocolonial and church influences continue to set a pattern for class and gender inequalities, and the economy
and politics remains dominated by powerful interest groups with strong interfamily connections. The education system is subject more to external than internal influences, teachers in particular being subject to centralised policies into
which neither they, nor teachers unions, have much input. There is, however, a
vibrant critique of the Maltese education system internally from university academics and some practitioners (see Bartolo, Ferrante, Azzopardi, Bason, Grech,
King 2002, Borg and Mayo 2006, Darmanin, 2002, 2003, 2010, Sultana, 1998,
2001, 2010). As in some larger capitalist countries education is increasingly subject to a neo-liberal market discourse, which supports social class inequalities in
schooling and subsequent placement in the economy. This chapter briefly covers
education policy in Malta with its continuing emphasis on selection of students
for different schools and classes, special and vocational education and the views
of participants with whom discussion took place. It concludes that while Malta
aims at developing a knowledge economy, this economy is not planned to include
lower attainers. While more attention has been paid to those with learning difficulties and low attainment, some 41 per cent of young people still drop out of
education at 16.

Malta is a small (316 square km) island with a population estimated at just under 406,800, added to annually by over a million tourists and a number of overseas students, mainly from around the Mediterranean and the EU. As it is near the North African coast it is also the destination of illegal migrants from Africa. Most of the main island is built over, and 94 per cent of the population are classed as urban. The island, colonised over the centuries by Romans, Normans, Arabs, Spain and France eventually became a British colony, and won the Victoria Cross for resisting invasion during the Second World War. It remained a major military base until the late 1960s and the economy was for a long time dependent on work in the naval and military garrison. It did not gain political independence until 1964. Malta finally became a Republic in 1974 and joined the European Union in 2004. A labour party (Social Democrat) held political power from 1971–1987, but apart from a brief spell in office in the mid-1990s the National Party (Christian Democrat) has held power for over 20 years. Party politics in Malta can be bitter, and educational politics can also be hostile. For example, in an article in *Malta Today* in 2010, the Minister of Education was accused by a Shadow Minister of 'running education like a personal fiefdom' and being incapable of showing any strategic leadership in education (Bartolo 2010a). The island is a Catholic country and church influence is strong, influencing education, family life and the place of women in the society. Sultana and Baldachino have written that 'Few have dared to systematically address the hegemony of the Catholic church in Malta . . . or the distribution of wealth among various groups' (Sultana and Baldachino 1994: 7). Gender issues figure large in a country where women have long been regarded as the pillar of family life and there is still no civil divorce. Unlike most other countries, girls have not outperformed boys in school examinations and are more likely to be in low-skill, low-wage jobs, although most say they want to combine work with family life (Darmanin 2009). A long report in 2006 from the National Commission for the Promotion of Equality, *Family-friendly measures in the workplace*, suggested ways in which women could achieve higher-grade employment, which in turn would help Malta and the EU become leading economies (NCPE 2006).

While from the 1970s the Labour Party sought to diversify the economy and move away from dependency on servicing the military, particularly towards manufacturing and the tourist industry, the National Party later declared its commitment to a 'knowledge economy'. The island was to become a centre for banking and finance, the ITC industries, gaming firms, pharmaceuticals, aviation maintenance and other innovations. In 2007 a centre for ITC and media, named 'Smart City' was designed near the capital Valletta, and international firms are represented there, several with particular links with Dubai and Gulf companies (Malta Smart Innovation 2011). How this helps the lower attainers is not clear. There is growing unemployment on the island, and half the unemployed are between 16–27, in 2009 17.6 per cent of these were male and 15.4 per cent female. For those who do not continue in education after 16 there is some work in the tourist, construction and other services, but as elsewhere, employers are increasingly demanding qualifications for even low-skilled jobs.

Education and selection

Historically the Maltese education system was heavily influenced by Britain who, as argued by Chircop (2001), collaborated with local elites and the Church, although officially there is a separation of Church and State. It was only in 1946, after a Compulsory Education Ordinance, that all children were required to attend school from 6–14. As an example of continuing neocolonial influence, in the later 1990s several of Prime Minister Tony Blair's advisers went to Malta to advise on education reorganisation, stressing the virtues of competition. One result of this was a clause in a 2007 Education Act allowing any person to open a school. The school system has a long history of selection of students at 11 with sporadic attempts to alter this. The National Party, originally a strong supporter of selection, has a close relationship with the Church and the Church still influences the national curriculum in all schools. A new national minimum curriculum for years 3–16 was notionally introduced from 1998, with the Church objecting to sex education, and it was also suggested at this time that lower achievers should be dealt with through after-school work, not in regular school hours.

The system is split between State schools, Church schools (mainly funded by the State and requiring students to pay for textbooks, and other resources) and some private schools, one Muslim school among these. In 2005 some 63.3 per cent of all students 3–16 were in State schools, 24.5 per cent in Church schools and 12.2 per cent in the private sector. Secondary schooling is predominantly in single-sex institutions and Darmanin (2007) has noted that while Pope John II praised women for their intellectual abilities and professionalism, more recent church pronouncements have attacked 'feminisms' and praised the values of motherhood and caring rather than employment opportunities. From 1946 students were selected at age 11 for the Lyceum (grammar school), technical school or general secondary school, and as elsewhere in selective systems it was largely the middle classes who dominated the grammar schools. In 1971 the Labour Party attempted to abolish selection and create mixed ability classes and develop comprehensive schools, but attempts at ending selection were abandoned in 1981, to be resurrected again in 2007. The selective system was to be reformed with students taking fewer tests at 11+ but still allocated to schools and classes on the basis of their results. The technical schools, as in the UK, gradually disappeared and in 1972 trade schools with vocational courses were established, with these too later phased out. From the nineteenth century British examinations dominated the system, Oxford and Cambridge examinations, Royal Society of Arts (RSA) and City and Guilds, but by 1994 Malta had developed its own school leaving certificates, the Malta Secondary Education Certificate (MSEC) at intermediate and advanced levels. Students are expected to learn Malti as well as English, the Maltese language still being common, especially among older people.

A reorganisation of the education system from 2007 divided the Island into ten areas, confusingly known as 'colleges', the island of Gozo being one college. Each area has a number of primary and secondary schools and parents can notionally choose schools. Each school is intended to have more administrative responsibility, but most funding and major administrative control remains with the central government, and there are suggestions that the appointment of 'college directors' is politically influenced. It is only State schools which fall into this 'college' reorganisation, Church schools and private schools not being included. In addition, the Church has permission to build new secondary schools for some 2000 boys, and as a consequence of the school choice agenda, parents are more than ever likely to choose Church and private schools. It is estimated that the state school sector will shrink to some 58 per cent of students. Lower attainers, especially boys, will be over-represented in the state sector as aspirant parents choose the historically middle class Church and grammar schools. For students who remain in education at 16 taking an academic route, two-year pre-university courses are offered at post-16 colleges. Church schools and private schools have their own academic post-16 courses, still funded by the State, which has no control over admissions. Teachers are mainly trained at the University of Malta on the three-year model of a degree plus a year's certificate, or the four year B.Ed, and recently a part-time course in early education has been introduced, as have Masters courses in special education and inclusion. There have been no large-scale studies of education and social class in Malta, but, as in the UK, evidence indicates that the education system services a social class system, in which the schools regarded as superior, the Church and private schools, are predominantly attended by middle-class students, and the general state schools by more working-class students. More middle-class students go on to higher education, especially in the prestigious University of Malta, while working-class students are more likely to attend vocational college. Baldachino (1993) noted that the terms middle and working class were a simplification of a complex and emerging class system, the pinnacle of a local economic class structure being a commercial elite with interfamily connections.

Special education

Special schools for children with disabilities were set up post-Second World War, but in 1989 the government promoted inclusive education with the intention of reducing numbers in special schools. In 1994 an inclusive education policy was officially introduced and the intention was that all students would have access to the Malta national curriculum. Again influenced by the UK, Learning Support Assistants (LSAs) were employed in mainstream schools. A Committee for Inclusive and Special Education, writing a review in 2005, pressed for the inclusion of as many children as possible in mainstream schools, and currently only around 200 attend the four special schools for severe learning difficulties, spending some time in mainstream schools if possible. Membership of the EU made it possible to claim additional funds from the European Social Fund for special education services. In 2007 a Student Services Department was set up with a director appointed to oversee all special services, and in 2008 service managers were appointed to deal with inclusive education, special resource centres and psychosocial services. In 2010 the Minister of Education announced a reform of special education, with the special schools now to be known as Resource Centres and integrated into the college system by area. Definitions of special education include 'those children who have special difficulties of a physical, sensory, intellectual or psychological nature'. They are assessed for a statement of special educational needs and fall into categories of intellectual disability, specific learning difficulty, emotional and behavioural difficulty, sensory difficulty, physical disability and multiple disability. (Ministry of Education, Culture and Sport 2010). Unofficial labels such as autism, ADHD and dyslexia are also in use.

As in other countries, major anxieties centre round the lower attainers included in mainstream schools, disruptive students, school drop outs and teen pregnancy, and attempts are made to deal with these largely through therapeutic measures. Increases in antisocial behaviour, bullying and other forms of social, emotional and behavioural problems in schools in Malta have been noted and a general view was that it was boys in state schools who were more likely to be disruptive, have learning problems and leave without qualifications. A variety of support services were available – the schools' psychological service, the education social work service, guidance and counselling services, anti-substance abuse services and others. In Malta, the therapeutic and counselling services have been supplemented by what Darmanin (2003) called 'love as an alternative discourse'. She noted that lower-achieving working-class students were offered love and care, in place of educational programmes, while middle class were prepared for a competitive market economy. The Ministry supported the idea of what was first described as 'Learning Zones', places where students with academic and behavioural problems could be internally excluded within schools, and helped to improve so that they could be reintegrated into the mainstream. The zones were based on the UK PRUs, and regarded as an alternative to straight exclusion from school. The *Times of Malta* (2009) reported that one of the first learning zones had opened to take in students with learning, social and behavioural problems. By 2010 Learning Zones were to be renamed Learning Centres, and the Ministry of Education claimed learning support centres and nurture groups would provide teaching and support for difficult and at-risk students and minimise the disruption to others caused by these challenging students.

Vocational education

Although currently the smallest country in the EU, Malta has adopted the goals set out in the Lisbon Agenda of free markets and belief in global competition, with a knowledge economy supposedly accompanied by flexible workers who will invest in their own human capital. Malta also, as in the UK, made assumptions that there is a skills crisis and shortage of skills, rather than a jobs crisis, where shortage of jobs is the problem. An employment strategy was set out in a national development plan from 2003 and political ambitions were for Malta to become a knowledge-driven economy by investing in, for example, ITC, micro-electronics, pharmaceuticals and other 'high value-added manufacturing and other service activities' (Central Bank of Malta 2006). What the position of lower attainers in this economy would be is not remarked on, and there is currently rising youth unemployment among the early leavers, although some young people leave school to work in family businesses. The trade schools developed from the 1970s and eventually joined with junior craft centres for lower achievers, were overtaken by apprenticeship schemes with students from age 14 with the equivalent of two years in school and two with an employer. More recently apprenticeships are available under a technical apprenticeship scheme and an extended skills training scheme overseen by an Employment Training Corporation, which arranges work placements but is organised by the Ministry of Education. In June 2010 the Minister of Education announced that curriculum changes would allow schools to prepare students pre-16 for BTEC qualifications in vocational subjects, with a pilot project to cover engineering, hospitality and social care. The announcement led to accusations from the teacher unions of lack of consultation, few teachers trained to teach these courses, and payment required for the course examinations (Calleja 2010). It is noteworthy that Malta was planning to introduce these BTEC courses at a time when in England the new Coalition Government was criticising the equivalence of vocational courses with academic subjects.

The main provider of all post-16 vocational education and training is the Malta College of Arts, Science and Technology (MCAST), set up in 2001, and which according to promotional literature has a mission to provide universally-recognised vocational and professional education and training, with an international dimension, responsive to the needs of the individual and the economy. Students can also enrol at a separate Institute of Tourism Studies and an Institute for Health Care. MCAST is made up of nine institutes located around the island: the Institute of Art and Design; the Community Service Institute, a Maritime Institute, the Institute of Information and Communications Technology, an Institute of Mechanical Engineering, an Institute of Business and Commerce, an Agribusiness Institute, an Institute of Electrical and Electronics Engineering and an Institute of Building and Construction. MCAST takes students at all levels of attainment and its qualifications include BTEC, City and Guilds, and international professional qualifications. A Malta National Qualifications Council was set up in 2005, and a National Qualifications Framework includes entry-level and foundation courses, leading on to eight levels with vocational education and training (VET) equivalents. Thus from lower attainers to doctoral degrees the courses include:

- Entry-level and foundation courses
- Level 1 General education school-leaving certificate (VET level 1)
- Level 2 General education SEC grades 1–7 (VET level 2)
- Level 3 General education SEC grades 1–5 (VET level 3)
- Level 4 Matriculation certificate – advanced and intermediate (VET diploma)

- Level 5 Undergraduate diplomas or certificates (VET diploma)
- Level 6 Bachelor degree
- Level 7 Master degree, postgraduate diploma
- Level 8 Doctoral degree.

The college principal declared his aim to be the integration of academic and vocational curricula, and from September 2010 the concept of 'embedded learning' was introduced. Maths, English, Malti, IT and personal development were to be embedded in all vocational courses. He wrote that

> Both the academic and the vocational have different organising principals and purposes which need to be reflected in the content and design of courses. We are looking at an alternative system based on the approach a number of countries like France and Germany have successfully implemented over the years, whereby vocational education is not seen as unjustifiably narrowing in its scope, rather the practical focus becomes the incentive to achieve high general educational standards.
>
> (Grech 2010)

MCAST is not without its critics. The Shadow Minister of Education noted in 2010 that although 5569 students started courses at the various institutes in 2009, by the end of the year 14 per cent had dropped out (13 per cent of these being female). The highest drop out rates were in electrical engineering and IT. It was also alleged that the teaching of courses was not well-regulated and there was scope for irregularities such as falsifying grades to claim higher rates of success (Bartolo 2010b).

Participants' views

Those who participated in discussion included the head teacher of a special school, where the area 'college director' was also visiting, the Director of the Student Services Department, his deputy and other staff in the Directorate, the Director of Information and Support Services at MCAST, and the principal of a sixth-form college. There was also some discussion with women studying for an MA in special and inclusive education.

The special school for 47 children with severe and multiple disabilities was well-equipped with almost 1:1 staffing, including parent volunteers. The school had a hydrotherapy pool, rooms for sensory experience with music and light, and young staff who were familiar with the latest technological aides. The head teacher approved of the policy aim of making the school a resource centre for other schools. Although, as in other countries, the concept of inclusion was contested and debatable she was clear that even the most severely disabled children should go into mainstream classes, if only for limited periods, as she thought this would have positive effects for all children. The issue of transporting children between schools to bring about 'inclusion' was as much an issue on this small island as in larger countries. The children all had statements of special needs and an individual education programme and there were guidelines for all special education teachers. As in England, there were issues over statementing, as parents want a statement and the extra resources this brings. Those with a statement whether in special or mainstream are entitled to a learning support assistant until 16. The visiting director described the recent area arrangements in more detail, in which there will be clusters of primary, secondary and a special school, claiming that parents would be given more choice of school, and schools have more autonomy. Despite these claims most funding, including teachers' salaries and capital building costs, will be retained by the centre and some funding going straight to the college director for distribution to schools. As in England, funding is based per capita on numbers of students and the director noted that this created competition between schools, including that between State, Church and private schools.

The Director of Student Services and his colleagues were housed in a large pleasant central building which also functioned as a centre for in-service training. There were a number of in-service courses in progress, including a class on language disabilities and second language learning, a class on new technologies and a masters-level class on inclusive education. The students on the course were mainly discussing the inclusion of more severely disabled children. The student services were organised and funded centrally and included educational psychologists, behavioural therapists, counsellors, speech and language services and careers guidance, with some funding for the services coming from the European Social Fund. The senior psychologist noted that the service was currently overloaded due to a rise in dyslexia, autism, including Asperger's syndrome and disruptive behaviour in schools. More referrals were coming from both schools and parents, and he considered that there were stronger links between poorer homes and poor parenting, with more child abuse, drug and alcohol abuse. The senior staff all were of the opinion that as there was a rise in social, emotional and behavioural disorders in schools, more psychologists, counsellors, behavioural therapists and behaviour management staff were needed. In the schools the Learning Zones, soon to be labelled Learning Centres (and described by some cynical teachers as 'Non-learning Centres'), were regarded as a way of keeping disruptive and lower-attaining students in school rather than excluding them, but there was no requirement to teach the national curriculum. There was notionally a transition service for young people with a statement of special needs, but staff said they found this difficult to implement. The careers service gave advice but those who dropped out of school or left completely at 16 were not followed up. The director noted that the school's drop out rate was disturbing, especially among girls, but some of the male lower attainers joined the military! As elsewhere, there were difficulties with smooth teamwork among the professionals, with problems in passing individual data around to different professionals.

At MCAST, the Director of Information and Support Services, based on the central campus, described the organisation of the college into the nine institutes, the recruitment of students at 16 or older, the qualifications to be achieved, and the arrangements for 'lower achievers' who 'often arrive having been labelled as failures'. The 145 courses which can be studied at MCAST provide qualifications which are adjusted to the Malta National Qualifications Framework, and qualifications range from a Pathway to Independent Living for those with moderate learning disabilities to the Certificate for Ships Chief Mate, equivalent to a degree at level 5. The college begins recruiting each July for October courses and prospective students and their parents attend talks on the courses offered, including the work experience on offer at home and abroad. An aim of the college is 'to get over to lower attainers that all can work'. Students with declared learning difficulties or disabilities can contact an Inclusive Education Unit for advice on courses and there a Learning Support Unit with a staff of 20. Lower-attaining students take tests on entry to check on functioning in literacy, numeracy and problem-solving and can enter on foundation courses, level 1 or level 2, and those with moderate difficulties go on the Pathways to Independent Living. Students can go on to level 2 vocational courses if they pass tests in English, Maths, Malti and IT, and the learning support staff help students with this and also take a lead in the embedded learning aimed at by the principal. The aim was for those on occupational courses to acquire literacy and numeracy skills as part of the courses rather than have these subjects separated from the vocational work. The director noted that employers like the idea that Maths, for example, was taught in a workshop rather than in a classroom, and a Foundation Certificate piloting embedded learning had just been introduced. The Learning Support Unit also supported students who have been 'diagnosed' as dyslexic, a senior lecturer explaining that

> dyslexia is a language-based, information-processing difficulty which causes problems in learning how to read, write and spell. Short-term memory, maths, concentration, organisation and sequencing can also be affected. Dyslexia occurs among the very bright, the average and the leas [*sic*] academically able . . . students with dyslexia are counselled and receive extra support to make it less likely that they experience educational failure.

The sixth-form college visited opened in 1984 to offer 'second chances' and revision courses to students wanting to continue with an academic education but with too few O-level subject passes – from British influence, the MSEC is still referred to as O, ordinary level. The college proved very popular, with some 1000 students in the 1990s and by 2010 around 2000 students attending, many from overseas. Some were from European countries, especially the former Yugoslavia, but there were also students from Brazil, China, Uzbekistan and other places. The college is well-resourced, all teachers are given laptop computers and all classrooms are connected to the Internet. Multicultural education was openly discussed and practised, and the Principal was very concerned about the situation of African migrants who on arrival were usually placed in camps around the island and could not participate in education. Unless they got a work permit they could not work and were left in difficult conditions which created conflicts with local people. Public policy discourages migrants from working, claiming that this creates unemployment among Maltese citizens (Sacco 2010). The school motto is 'Another chance in life' and offers one-year academic revision courses. Those with four O-level subjects can study for one or two years for the Matriculation Certificate which gives entry to university. Although learning support officially ends at 16, the college is able to provide learning support assistance to the small number of students who come with an IEP, and has a disability policy, and a diversity and equality policy designed for all students. All students take enrichment courses ranging from communications, drama and entrepreneurship to guitar-playing, garden management and personal growth and leadership, and there is compulsory sports. The college participates in European projects, currently a Comenius project which involves visits with schools in Finland, Germany, Greece and Italy, and Euroscuola sessions at the European Parliament in Strasbourg. As with other post-16 institutions in Malta, efforts are made to involve parents in their children's education and future. A careers and counselling team meet students and parents before registration and organise parent evenings. Recent themes were 'Parental fears regarding their young adult seeking independence' and 'Parental conflict'.

Conclusions

The education system in Malta is still heavily influenced by its British colonial past and has embraced the market-oriented competitive notions of schooling advocated by English policy makers and advisers, which leads to social class separation. This fits in well with the traditional orientation towards selection, as even if the 11+ is eventually removed, 'choice' of school will continue to benefit the Church and private schools historically dominated by the middle classes. A counter influence is that, since joining the EU, Malta is also influenced by other European countries and their education systems, especially post-16 vocational education. However, the Maltese government has enthusiastically embraced the notion that education must be geared towards a knowledge economy, and the development of new industries, plus the selective system and selective entry to this knowledge economy, continues to benefit elite groups. As in other countries, it is accepted that while all social classes can produce children with more severe disabilities, it is the lower-class lower-attaining children, with their labels of disruptive, social, emotional and behavioural disorders, who are regarded as most problematic. Over the past 20 years more attention has been paid to this group, who are the most likely to be school drop outs and early leavers, and policies for inclusive education encourage the retention of those with learning difficulties and disruptive behaviour in schools, but via separate learning centres. There is, in common with other countries, a growing realisation that all young people must be educated and trained for some kind of employment, but as elsewhere the rhetoric of a knowledge economy precludes much planning for the employment of lower attainers. As these are largely from lower-class families, major anxieties centre round the social control of potentially rebellious young people. Although the Church and family have historically had a strong controlling influence on young people, there is a recognition that this is diminishing. As elsewhere, in Malta the psychological and therapeutic professions have expanded their staffing and influence. Their main function is to assess, counsel and guide young people into approved social behaviour at school and at home. While some student problems are given the more acceptable labels, dyslexia, Asperger's and so on, which are regarded as 'treatable' and given resources, it is those who acquire the labels associated with disruption and disaffection who are candidates for disapproval and exclusion.

Some educators admit that the selective system encourages lower attainers to regard themselves as failures, but selection continues after 16, when it is lower class and lower attainers who leave early and with few qualifications. Those on the borderline of achieving the Secondary Certificate and going on to higher education are encouraged to repeat and retake examinations at sixth-form institutors, others are encouraged to take up apprenticeships and the MCAST offers a range of courses for lower attainers to start at low-entry levels and progress to other courses. The notion of 'embedded learning' in vocational courses may prepare those students who, as in other countries, are resistant to learning in traditional classrooms, but the structural elaboration of the education system to cater for most lower achievers still takes the form of courses and more courses which do not necessarily lead on to employment. While other countries – Finland, Germany, France and the Netherlands, for example – make more effort to equip all students with a recognised vocational qualification and a trade, Malta, as in the UK, has little coherent planning for lower attainers and their future remains increasingly problematic.

Chapter 8

Finland

A model for us all?

The Finnish school system is thus an institution for disrupting the transmission of inequality in life chances from one generation to the next.
(Sabel, Saxenian, Miettinen, Kristensen, Hautamäki 2010: 2)

Here come more educational tourists!
(Helsinki head teacher 2011)

International comparative tests of student performances have become common around the world since 1958 when a group of scholars, including Martti Takala from Finland, developed an International Association for the Evaluation of Educational Achievement. Other large-scale international comparative tests were soon introduced: the PISA tests developed by the OECD for students aged 15 in reading, maths and science becoming the best known. The results of testing in 2001, 2003, 2006 and 2009, has led to continued anxieties on the part of governments who worry if their students go down in test scores, and educational policies in a number of countries have been influenced by PISA results. Finland, outperforming all other countries in the first three studies, rapidly became the country where the educational tourists described above – government policy makers, educational practitioners, researchers – flocked to examine how these good results were achieved, and to carry often simplified or controversial stories back to compare with their own education systems. The one indisputable result was that in Finland the lowest quintile of student achievers (lower attainers and special needs students) obtained higher scores than similar groups in any other countries. So, if Finland can prepare all young people, including lower attainers, to achieve higher levels, should Finland really become a model for other school systems? This chapter briefly discusses the development of Finnish education policy and PISA results, the arrangements for special and vocational education, the views of a small number of participants with whom discussion took place, and concludes that while Finland does indeed have much to teach other countries about a successful system which is egalitarian and does well for lower attainers, there are also similar problems to those experienced by other countries, especially in the fit between education and the labour market.[1]

Like Malta, Finland, with a current population of some 5.4 million, has a history of colonisation. The country was part of the Kingdom of Sweden from the thirteenth century to 1809, when it became part of the Russian Empire as the Grand Duchy of Finland. It only achieved independence as a separate country in 1917, although it lost a province (Karelia) back to Russia in the Second World War. Also like Malta the country has a dominant religion, 78 per cent of the population being Lutheran, and until recently politics, dominated by centrist and social democratic parties, appeared relatively uncontroversial. The True Finns party – a right-wing populist party which is anti-EU and anti-immigrant – usually obtained a small number of votes, but in the April 2011 election the True Finns vote rose to 19 per cent, causing concern that the party would turn disadvantaged Finns against immigrants (Six Degrees 2011). The immigrant population is in fact around 5 per cent, mainly Russian, Estonian, Somalian and from the former Yugoslavia; and Finnish children learn Swedish in schools. Despite True Finn hostility, giving additional teaching to immigrant children usually brings them up to required levels for mainstream classes, something 'which appears to have been overlooked by the educational tourists' (Shepherd 2011). The European-wide recession of the early 1990s caused unemployment in Finland, but the country currently has a relatively stable economy with, alongside other Nordic countries, the highest GDP per head of the populations of all the OECD countries. The country, well-known as an egalitarian social democracy with a poverty rate calculated at 4 per cent of the population (22 per cent and rising in the USA) is capitalist. The economy is based on industry – shipbuilding, especially cruise liners, metal working, some coal mining, car making, forestry, especially pulp and paper-making, and agriculture – with the 'knowledge economy' represented by communications (especially Nokia phones), electronics and the professions. As elsewhere service workers are required in health care, tourism, hotels and food and drink production. While unemployment for adults remains around the EU average, youth unemployment, as in other countries, continues to be problematic. The United Nations Office of Statistics report that in 2009 overall 20.5 per cent of young people 15–24 were unemployed, with more males (22 per cent) than females (18.8 per cent) unemployed. As some 96 per cent of young people 16–19 are in upper secondary school or initial vocational education, these figures would largely refer to 19–25 year olds. However, youth unemployment, especially in central and northern parts of Finland, is an issue worrying government. The *Nordic Labour Journal* reported in 2011 that the 'Finnish Presidency continues to fight against youth unemployment' (Linden 2011: 1) with a series of strategies for high skills training, lifelong learning and identifying business needs.

Education policies

The core of Finnish education policy is a commitment to comprehensive education and the comprehensive school – peruskoulu.[2] The education system is based on a belief that all young people need to have free and equal access to education to the highest possible level. Government decisions concerning money and resources take this principle into account and particular attention is given to children from less-educated lower-class homes, although a vocabulary of social class is eschewed in government and research literature. Most children attend their neighbourhood school, and although the concepts of choice and school evaluation were introduced in a 1991 Act, this has had little effect and there is little difference between schools in terms of student achievement. Although pressured by global economic forces Finland has not embraced the neo-liberal notion of competitive market choice between schools, or succumbed to a rhetoric of a knowledge economy, the system aiming to prepare young people at all levels for the economy. One explanation for the good levels of achievement may be a traditional respect for the (very well educated) teachers at all educational levels, and a culture of trust between political leaders, education authorities and parents, who, unlike in the UK and USA in particular, all appear to believe that teachers know how to provide the best education for children (Simola 2005, Sahlberg 2007). There are no school inspectors and no national-level testing. The education system is decentralised, with some 336 municipalities controlling education in their areas, and a National Board of Education setting out broad aims and contents for the basic curriculum, but the municipalities can modulate their own curriculum based on the national core. Kindergarten is available but not compulsory and at six children begin a pre-school year, entering the first grade at seven. Primary education lasts for 6 years and at around 13 students transfer to lower secondary school until 16, then to either an academic upper secondary or vocational schools/colleges until 19. Transfer between courses is possible and students from both types of institutions can go on to university or polytechnic or into employment. The attention given to students through what is still called special education (see below) but is more a form of intense individual additional attention and teaching from the early years, undoubtedly raises standards of achievement. The assumption is that schools, teachers and other professionals, together with adequate funding not additional handouts, are responsible for helping all children to achieve, rather than adhering to the deficit models of children and families common in other countries.

The current educational system was not achieved without much debate and argument, especially over selection and different types of school. Although compulsory education was introduced in 1921 and was based on social democratic principles. there was a long tradition of parallel separate schooling and 'ability streaming', and centralisation of the system. Up to the 1960s there was a demand for more selective grammar schools. But most countries, including Finland, were by the 1960s recognising that global economic changes and social justice claims needed more young people educated to higher levels, 'human capital' had become a buzz word, and it was clear that selecting a few for a superior education did not help the economy or social justice. A 1970 Act ushered in nine years of compulsory comprehensive schooling but still with in-school tracking/streaming, and some exclusion of students with disabilities and learning difficulties. It was not until

1985 that the education system was decentralised, with more autonomy given to municipalities and schools, ability grouping abolished, and extra money given to guarantee smaller teaching groups. From the 1970s teacher education in universities, but with partnerships with schools, was made a priority and all teachers are required to have a five-year training and a Masters degree (six years for special education teachers). In 1994 the National Board of Education further reduced its role in deciding the aims and content of the curriculum so that local needs and school characteristics could be considered (Laukkanen 2008), and as Graham and Jahnukainen concluded (2011), it was not until 1997 that the Finnish 'education for all' reforms were complete, when responsibility for the most severely disabled students moved from the social welfare services to education services. A Basic Education Act in 1998 required an individual education plan for all students requiring extra support, and all students, whatever their disability, had a right to enrol in their local school.

PISA tests

Although different countries have created education systems which depend on their histories and purposes – a major intention in the UK, in contrast to Finland, being to retain and reproduce elites – by the twenty-first century governments mostly had bought into the notion that in the global economy their countries needed a system in which all students, whatever their backgrounds, achieved higher levels in literacy, numeracy and science. Testing, especially in these subject areas, became an essential tool for comparison with economic competitors. The PISA tests, owned and developed by the OECD (who decide on questions and rankings), seemed an ideal tool for comparisons which has had considerable impact on policy makers in various countries (see Baird, Isaacs, Johnson, Stobart, Yu, Sprague et al. 2011). Finland astonished the world and itself when its sample of 15-year-old students performed the best in reading, maths and science in 2001, 2003 (from which England was excluded for 'over-testing' students) and 2006, with Canada, Hong Kong-China and Korea not far behind. In the 2009 tests Finnish students again performed best, although the global media made much of students in Shanghai whose reading scores came out as two points higher. In fact the Chinese government had put 12 provinces in for the tests but only released the results of Shanghai, which perhaps illustrates the nervousness of governments at appearing to fall behind in the competitiveness stakes. There are also questions around the selection of students for the tests, but Finnish students not only included lower attainers in their sample, all the students had only been in school for nine years, as opposed to ten in most other countries.

In 2008 Hautamäki and his colleagues produced for the Ministry of Education and Science an exhaustive account of the PISA results to 2006. The Minister herself wrote in the foreword that 'The intention is to open up the Finnish education system for those who wish to understand what OECD's PISA programme tells us about Finnish schooling . . . education is greatly valued in

Finland and we have highly competent and motivated teachers' (Foreword in Hautamäki, Harjunen, Hautamäki, Karjalainen, Kupiainen, Laarsonen *et al.* 2008). She also noted that the issue of how to deal with variations in learning between students 'had a moral aspect which has been recognised at the core of Finnish education policy'. Education For All in Finland, as the Minister noted 'has established a unified and comprehensive schooling to benefit persons, family, country and mankind', and the idea of education for all has resulted in special attention being given to children from less-educated families. Hautamäki and his colleagues briefly examined the history of education from the 1960s, compared the PISA results in the 30 countries which participated in 2006, and discussed the testing as a tool for comparing education systems. They also analysed in detail the Finnish performance, goals and curriculum in science, maths and reading, noting especially the between-school and in-school variations in student performance in these subjects. They demonstrated that as between-school variance was low, parents need to be less concerned about choice between schools. This certainly removes the need for the insane competition for the 'best' students in order to become the 'best' schools, which characterises countries which have turned schooling into a competitive market commodity.

Hautamäki concluded that the exceptional PISA results reflected an education system which has moved towards a more open and self-governed system, which has a strong emphasis on literacy and numeracy for all. The social and economic impact of homes and families on learning and testing is smaller than in the other countries. The country has the least number of obligatory tests for students among the PISA countries and yet the students cope well with the tests. However, the testing takes place before students have been guided towards their upper secondary education in either academic or vocational institutions or to different curricula, and although funding is generous, Finland is not the highest spender on education in relation to GDP in all other OECD countries. In terms of gender, as in other countries girls outperform boys in reading, boys slightly outperform girls in the maths tests, and in 2006 both performed equally well in science. A major conclusion is that good performance for all is largely due to the high quality of teachers, the teaching profession being respected and only around 10 per cent of those wanting to enter teacher education are accepted (Hautamäki, Harjunen, Hautamäki, Karjalainen, Kupiainen, Laarsonen *et al.* 2008: 203). There is no evidence from Finland that competitive markets between schools increases performance, or that students are less well prepared for a global market economy. Indeed Finland has been ranked as among the most competitive economies in the world. While the authors of the report acknowledge that policies cannot easily be transferred between countries, reports from educational visitors on Finnish schooling are often criticised for comparing the system favourably with their own. An online article by American scholar Ravitch (2011) praising Finnish schooling was followed by many critical responses claiming that the size and diversity of the American population and its schooling, plus its poverty levels, precluded adopting Finnish models.

Special education

As Sabel and colleagues (2010) have noted, it is the bottom quintile (20 per cent) of PISA test takers who outperform those in other countries, thus raising the mean scores to the top of international league tables. Parental socio-economic background is less likely to have an influence on scores, and parents of lower-achieving students are less likely to be blamed for their children's attainments than anywhere else. There is no academic or government literature suggesting that genetic inheritance or 'deprived' brains are barriers to learning. A major reason identified for this is the special educational services, or more accurately, the additional educational support, that some 30 per cent of students of all ages receive, which raises potential lower attainers to higher levels of learning. This, as Graham and Jahnukainen have commented (2011: 276) 'is undoubtedly a kind of unofficial world record'. Up to 2008 some 22 per cent of these students were in a part-time form of special education in mainstream schooling, 8 per cent in full-time special classes in mainstream, or in separate schools on a campus with mainstream schools and 2 per cent with the most severe learning difficulties likely to be in the special schools.[3]

It was a commitment to comprehensive schooling and its ending of streaming/tracking, that created the need for what Sabel and colleagues (2010: 26) called 'customized pedagogy' in which children who encounter learning difficulties or disaffection at various times in their school career, are given extra support by highly qualified special education teachers. The identification of children with possible learning difficulties or disabilities starts early, via a network of child health clinics staffed by trained professionals and free assessments of all pre-school children. Jahnukainen has noted that amendments to the Basic Education Act define special education in three tiers: general support, intensified support and special support (Jahnukainen 2012). In school the progress of children and their services is monitored by a Student Welfare Group (SWG) which reviews the performances of classes and students each year and identify those needing the part-time additional special attention. This requires a number of professionals to work together and, as elsewhere, 'smooth teamwork' is often difficult. There are different ways of organising special education, in mainstream it may take the form of individual attention, small group teaching or with team teaching, and the past ten years has seen an expansion of inclusive education. Some students may attend separate schools on a campus with mainstream schools, and some special schools take children from pre-school to 15 years, preparing them for transfer to mainstream and to vocational colleges. All those in special education have an IEP which is detailed and monitored. The students are recipients of a variety of special services, welfare services, guidance and counselling, special aids and teaching materials, all of which is expensive.

Although Finland never developed national standardised tests and does not publish information that would allow for the ranking of schools, Finnish children are regularly subject to diagnostic, formative tests to check on progress and learning problems. Teachers, researchers and professional test designers collaborate to produce tests and the remedial teaching materials needed. Some eight universities have research centres which carry out research in special education, assessment, child development and educational psychology. Free learning programmes, including computer-based learning games, are available for pre-school children, mostly developed in universities. One result of all the extra attention is that children do not have to 'wait to fail' before they get additional support (Graham and Jahhukaninen 2011: 278). However, as in other countries, an increase in the number of children offered special education worries government, and one researcher has referred to developments as 'an elephant with special needs' (Hautamäki, personal communication 2011). Over the past few years the number of students in full-time special education has gradually increased to around 8.5 per cent of the school population, and those in part-time special education increased to 23 per cent, with much local variation in numbers. Suggested reasons for this increase are the demand for an expansion of services from parents, the entry of new ethnic groups, more behavioural problems and student awareness of their insecure futures (Sabel, Saxenian, Miettinen, Kristensen, Hautamäki 2010: 49). Although all political parties agree that the society has an obligation to the Finnish vision of the best Education for All, there is disagreement about the form this should take.

Vocational education

After completing lower secondary school, at 16 some 55 per cent of students go on to upper secondary schools and around 40 per cent into initial vocational education and training colleges, the majority of lower attainers and special students attending these, which include a small number of special vocational colleges and training centres. Those attending the academic upper secondary schools take a subject-based course culminating in a matriculation certificate, after which they can progress to university. Under an Upper Secondary Schools Act of 1998, students in need of special support are entitled to special welfare and teaching services, and the most common claim is for dyslexia. There is a joint application procedure for the two types of institution, vocational colleges taking students on the basis of their school performance, possible previous work experience and sometimes an aptitude test. Students and their parents are consulted and counselled. Employers can take on apprentices from 16 with time split between the workplace and college, although most apprenticeships are for older workers. As in Germany and other Nordic countries, vocational colleges (governed by a Vocational Education Act 1998) are well-organised and well-resourced and their qualifications can lead on to degrees taken in a polytechnic.[4]

The Ministry of Education lays out the structure of vocational qualifications and the National Board of Education decides the core curriculum and assessment, all in collaboration with training committees which include employers. There are eight sectors of vocational education and training: humanities, culture, natural sciences, natural resources and environment, health and sports, social sciences and business studies, technology, communications and transport and some 52 actual qualifications. Students complete 120 credits over three years, 90 of these being vocational studies and training on the job, 20 in languages, maths and science, and 10 free-choice. All students who complete their vocational courses thus have a recognised qualification and can find employment, carry on in vocational adult courses or go on to a polytechnic. As in other countries there is a problem with those who drop out from college courses – in 2009 around 10 per cent of students – and the Ministry of Education has commissioned a study to enquire into reasons for this and try to reduce drop out rates (Jappinen 2010). Finland is, however, an enthusiastic participant in an annual World Skills competition, in which 56 countries now participate. Young workers with manual skills are selected to represent their countries in 45 skill areas. A member of the Finnish National Board of Education is a representative for the World Skills Foundation, and a research project initiated in 2007 at the Research Centre for Vocational Education at the University of Tampere (MoVE, Modelling of Vocational Excellence) explores the benefits of competition on skills formation (Nokelainen 2011).

Whether competition in acquiring vocational skills is an incentive for students with learning difficulties and disabilities is debatable, but the students may go to the ordinary vocational college, usually after counselling and discussion with the college special education teachers, or to one of the eight special vocational colleges taking students with more severe difficulties. One school in Oulu, for example, advertises that it takes children and young people who are disabled or neurologically impaired, including deaf, hard of hearing and those with autistic spectrum disorders. The arrangements for those with learning difficulties and/or disabilities is not regarded as satisfactory, Sabel and his colleagues remarking that 'The Finns have not yet reproduced or stumbled on successful solutions in domains where they are plainly needed – continuing vocational training for vulnerable groups in the society' (Sabel, Saxenian, Miettinen, Kristensen, Hautamäki 2010: 59).

Participants' views

Those who participated in discussions of lower attainers and special education in Finland included the head and special education teachers from two special schools on a campus which included a mainstream primary/lower secondary school and an upper secondary school, the principal of an upper secondary school, two special education teachers at a vocational college, and a seminar was organised at the School of Behavioural Sciences, University of Helsinki with researchers in the special education field.

One of the two special schools sharing a campus took pupils from pre-school to ninth grade, as their compulsory education lasted for eleven years instead of nine. All pupils in the mainstream are assessed on starting school at seven, and if learning problems are apparent, will move to this school. The basic studies were the same as in mainstream school but with a maximum of eight pupils per class.

The 60 pupils, which included some immigrant children, had a variety of mild and moderate learning difficulties, including specific language impairments, and sign language was used where necessary. The second school took students from seventh–ninth grade with a maximum of ten pupils in a class. The curriculum in this school was the same as in the mainstream school but with additional help in basic education. It was described as taking pupils with 'broad-based learning difficulties'. The head teacher was head of both schools and the motto for both schools was 'keep it simple'. Both schools were light, airy, well-decorated and resourced, all teachers had special education qualifications, and teaching assistants, welfare and psychological services were available. The teachers were highly professional and discussed their pupils in terms of teaching and learning theories as well as the practices adopted. In discussion it emerged that there was some hostility from mainstream teachers towards special education teachers as 'they are regarded as superior and get better pay'. This is an interesting inversion of views of special education teachers in the UK, for example, where historically it was less well-qualified teachers who taught children with learning difficulties and were regarded as less important. In all visits in the various countries coffee was usually served in discussions. In Finland this was accompanied by cake, in these schools it was blueberry cake! All students in education 6–19 are entitled to a free school meal and cafeterias, advised by dieticians, produce nourishing food (no French fries!). The pupils at these two schools join in sports, including matches against the staff: on this visit pupils beat the teachers in a rounders (baseball) match, and the young children play in common playgrounds with those from the other schools. In the transition to upper secondary level there is much guidance and counselling for all students in conjunction with the students and their parents, and most went on to vocational education and training either in the ordinary colleges and those with more severe learning disabilities to special vocational colleges.

In the upper secondary school the principal (who has a doctorate) held an early meeting with all staff to thank two who were retiring, and offered coffee and cream cakes to all. Although the school was well-organised and the 400 students purposefully engaged, especially as they were shortly to receive results of their matriculation exam, the principal noted that it was not in the top percentage of academic schools. Although the language of social class is not used, he indicated that the students were from working-class homes, and some of the students were immigrant, mainly from other European countries. The students at this school were more likely to be going on to polytechnics than university. The whole school assembled in the hall for a play, written and acted by the students, and an examiner from a drama college attended to observe a student who had applied for entry. The theme of the play was the dangers of drink, drugs, violence and sex, and as the principal remarked, these themes were common to young people in many countries and there was no need to translate from the Finnish! In discussion the amount of alcohol consumed in Finland was raised, both as a problem for adults and young people, and there had been an increase in babies born with foetal alcohol syndrome which caused mental health and learning problems.

The vocational college visited was north of Helsinki, part of a consortium of colleges in the area. Of the 5,000 students admitted in 2009 to the eight colleges 15.7 per cent were officially classed as special education students. Two special education teachers discussed the work of the college and their students. One was about to apply to study for a doctorate, and the other teacher spoke four languages. Again, they mentioned that other teachers were often wary of special education teachers as they are better qualified and better paid. Of the 600 students attending this college for 16–24-year-olds, some 120 were regarded as having special needs and had an IEP. While these could include those assessed as having autism, dyslexia, ADHD, hearing or vision problems, it was left to the students to self-declare if they needed additional special help, especially with literacy and numeracy. It was noted that some students were embarrassed about this and did not seek help until they were falling behind. Students are still required to learn Swedish which creates problems as students do not want to learn the language, although this requirement is under review. Although the teachers were not familiar with the term 'lower attainers' they took the view that it was students with mild learning problems and poor behaviour who 'are the main problem for the college'. Those with more severe problems or 'intellectually disabled' are in separate colleges. The students were studying for one of 19 vocational diplomas, which includes both practical work and academic subjects. The courses available include bakery and confectionery, chef, construction, light engineering, motor vehicle maintenance, care and home services, hotel and tourism, laboratory work, and practical nursing. The students spend 20 weeks in work experience either in a block or on day-release. There were no hair and beauty courses, young people wishing to do this learned on the job. It was noted that the vocational special education colleges are 'for those who need special support in their studies and in subsequent placement'. One of these colleges advertised itself as having 'a versatile range of special needs education working closely with practical training providers and providing all learners with the competence and skills they will need in the future'. The college offers support to both young people and adults after students take up work.[5]

Conclusions

The attention given to lower attainers and students with learning problems undoubtedly contributes to the good PISA results, and at all levels of their school careers the students probably experience more attention from a variety of professional and highly trained teachers, than in any other country. The egalitarian assumption that all young people are to be valued, whatever their learning difficulties, and educated to the highest possible levels to 19 or older, influences national and local policies, and the well-qualified teachers, who are highly regarded and professional, a variety of other qualified professionals, and good resourcing contributes to the aim of better levels of education and training for all.

Although it is often assumed abroad that all children and young people are in one mainstream school with additional help, in fact there are a variety of ways in which the 'special education' or additional help is given, including in separate facilities. This does not negate the whole belief in a comprehensive education for all, and adequate preparation for all young people for a working life.

However, as in other countries there are problems. Although it is not openly discussed and the language of social class is not much used, there is, as elsewhere, a difference in destinations for those from middle-class and working-class homes. The latter and those with low attainments and learning difficulties are more likely to be in vocational colleges after 16 and prepared for service employment rather than professional or 'knowledge economy' jobs. This appears to be the destination for many immigrant children, although they get additional help in schools. Although all students who complete their courses are qualified for a job, the global recession in 2008 had affected Finland, and there were fewer jobs available. As in other countries, there is a lack of congruence between education, vocational training and the labour market, and youth unemployment is regarded as a major problem by government. There is a lack of information on the kinds of jobs available locally and regionally for lower attainers, apart from assumptions that their employment will be lower-skilled and lower-waged, and that some of those with more severe disabilities may have to be permanently supported by the state. It is also the case that students who are lower attainers and are badly behaved, are more likely to be regarded as problematic, forming the majority of drop outs from schools and colleges, and there are problems with excessive alcohol consumption among many young people.

Few other countries can currently match the egalitarianism in Finnish society, which, however imperfect, underpins the philosophy of a comprehensive education for all which is not simply rhetoric. The nearest the UK came to this view was in the late 1960s/early 1970s when moves towards non-selective secondary education, the beginnings of inclusion of those with difficulties and disabilities, and the highest levels of expenditure on education ever, caused one social historian to comment that 'educational forms embodying a new human perspective might be made a reality' (Simon 1991: 405). However, this did not happen and there was a swift retrenchment from egalitarian educational policies. While aspects of the Finnish education system could become a 'model for us all', the belief that schooling must be a competitive enterprise serving a competitive global economy is firmly fixed in the policies adopted in the UK and many other countries, and it is unlikely that this will change in the near future.

Notes

1 This chapter drew on information provided in the extensive analysis of PISA 2006 (Hautamäki, Harjunen, Hautamäki, Karjalainen, Kupiainen, Laarsonen 2008) and of Sabel and colleagues (2010) on special education. Special thanks to Professor Jarkko Hautamäki, Department of Applied Sciences, University of Helsinki and Dr Reeta Mietola, KUFE, Department of Education, University of Helsinki.

2 Translations, especially from Finnish, are notoriously problematic, as Hautamäki and Hautamäki explain (Hautamäki, Harjunen, Hautamäki, Karjalainen, Kupiainen, Laarsonen 2008: 27). The original comprehensive school was described as peruskoulu, roughly a basic institution. The idea was that all children would attend their nearest school mixing with others from the same area, at primary (alakoulu) and lower secondary levels. Divisions into upper secondary institutions were not intended to be associated with early selection and different destinations but was part of a good basic education for all citizens while recognising student variation, and giving equal resources and esteem.

3 Those qualifying for full-time special education were described from 2002 as having: severely delayed development; slightly delayed development; physical disability/cerebral dysfunction; emotional disturbance/social maladjustment; visual or hearing impairment; and learning difficulties related to autism/Asperger's syndrome or impaired linguistic development.

4 Polytechnic, institute of technology and university of applied science mean the same thing in Finland. There are currently 27 of these, with 10 multidisciplinary universities and six specialist universities in music, drama, arts and technology.

5 The colleges discussed are Omnia college in the Espoo area and Luovi College in Oulu.

Chapter 9

Conclusions

Low attainers, low-skill work and flexicurity

This book set out to consider how lower attainers are currently defined in developed countries, what is happening to the young people in terms of their education and training post-14, what sort of courses and programmes are in place for them, and how they fit into a 'knowledge economy'. Historically, lower attainers in education systems, whether as recipients of minimal education, special education, mainstream or inclusive education, have also been the recipients of denigration, paternalistic or punitive benevolence, dominated by fear of their disruptive potential. From the late nineteenth century efforts were made to make sure that all who were potential lower attainers in education, or were likely to be a burden on the State through their disabilities, were prepared if possible for some kind of low-level work, and the social control of potentially disruptive young people was crucial. Currently it has become part of a more intense ideology that all young people should become economically productive in some way, and not reliant on unemployment or welfare benefits. While engaging in a rhetoric of a knowledge economy in which those with higher levels of knowledge are privileged, governments have also insisted that all young people, whatever their difficulties, disability or disengagement, should participate in more and more education and training and gain some sort of qualification. The rationale for this is that higher levels of education and skills training for all are necessary for successful national competition in a global economy, and there are increasing anxieties that many of the young people will become part of a 'surplus population' in knowledge economies. There is less focus on restructuring economies or producing policies that will create jobs and thus prevent unemployment. Yet it is predominantly through social and economic policies rather than individual deficits, that young people come to be unemployed or placed at lower levels with low wages in the labour market. High levels of 'knowledge' may be required to join the knowledge economy, although it may be the case, as Brown and colleagues (2011) have pointed out, that Western countries have yet to realise that their assumed superior position in the global knowledge economy is threatened. Ha-Joon Chang has also suggested that in rich countries 'their obsession with higher education has to be tamed' as the link between higher education and national productivity is tenuous and distorts the rest of the economy (Ha-Joon Chang 2011: 188). But the current political assumption is that all must aim to join this knowledge economy and there is a persistent punitive and paternalistic view of social groups who are unlikely to attain higher levels of knowledge. Although there is little evidence that young lower attainers are the 'ignorant yobs' portrayed in some sections of the media and in government policy in Britain[1] or that they are unwilling to work, the young people are subject to, at the very least, a lack of serious attention and at worst, constant denigration. This particularly applies to black and some other minority young people. This chapter draws some conclusions to this study of those dealing with the young people in five countries, and suggests a model in which lower attainers might fit into labour markets in developed countries.

Expanded education systems

Education systems in developed countries have steadily expanded over the past 100 years, but over the past 20 years expansion has accelerated. At the top end there has been a large increase in numbers entering higher education, with the assumption that its graduates are mainly destined for a knowledge economy and high-level employment. At the lower end, those who were previously excluded, or offered a minimum or a special education have been drawn into lower-level education and training schemes with the assumption that they will fill low-level, low-wage jobs, but that these now need some kind of qualification. Definitions of lower attainers by participants in this study ranged from those who did not obtain requisite passes in academic exams at 16, obtain high school diplomas or secondary leaving certificates, have problems acquiring numeracy and literacy and/or have mild, moderate or severe learning difficulties or disabilities. While numbers in these groups varied between schools, regions and countries an average of those considered to be lower attainers appeared to be 25 per cent. In England the official percentage was 21 per cent for those with special educational needs, with variations between schools and areas of up to 40 per cent for those with learning problems. Half of all young people at 16 did not attain the benchmark of five GCSEs. In the USA the 15–20 per cent of those regarded as having a learning disability were a particular focus for attention, although some schools classed half their students as learning disabled. In Germany those who left the Hauptschule or special school without a certificate and moved into a transition system were regarded as a problem, as were the 40 per cent in Malta who leave education at 16 with few or no qualifications. While Finland offered additional educational help to nearly a quarter of students, the expectations that all will progress to a more equal academic or vocational education after 16 reduced the need for a concept of 'lower attainer', although around 8 per cent of more severely disabled students have special arrangements. In all the countries it was the lower attainers who made up the majority of students on lower-level vocational courses in schools and colleges, and were likely to be from lower social classes and minority groups. While the rhetoric of a knowledge economy does not include much recognition of the continued necessity for the services of the low-skilled, governments are now prepared to encourage the preparation of those who will do necessary lower-skilled and manual jobs by funding assistance if targets are met, and – although there are current anxieties over the uses and abuses of special education – professional assistance for those who have trouble gaining adequate levels of certification. This is the case in both centralised and decentralised systems. Extended provision for all lower attainers, however described, continues to be primarily economic – all must join the labour force if possible. It also continues to be a mechanism for the social control of large groups of young people who potentially could be disruptive to the wider society. This is illustrated by the control of disruptive behaviour in schools by time-out rooms, pupil referral units, support schools, schools for social, emotional and behavioural problems, behaviour management programmes, exclusion and expulsion, personal and social development programmes and the expansion of psychological, medical and therapeutic professions to deal with the young people.

Special, mainstream and vocational

It was Lawrence Mead, whose writing influenced welfare-to-work legislation in the USA, who claimed that paid employment was an obligation of citizenship (Mead 1986). This is a serious charge, because it assumes that those who find difficulty in reaching required levels of education and training for paid work cannot satisfy the requirements for citizenship. It also leaves aside any obligations the State might have to provide work. Nevertheless, since all young people are expected to achieve some kind of qualification and join the labour market, the separation of special and mainstream education becomes problematic. The ideology and practice of inclusive education has brought into mainstream schools and colleges large numbers of young people with learning difficulties and disabilities, who would previously have been segregated in special schools and classes, joining fellow students once regarded simply as slow-learning lower attainers. Pressures on public comprehensive schools are more intense, with the expectation that all young people will achieve some kind of qualification. In the main, schools and colleges have responded to these pressures positively, but a major consequence of these expectations has been an expanded and expensive 'special education industry'. Young people who are lower attainers or have learning difficulties in mainstream and special schools are recipients of an army of teaching and learning support assistants, inclusive education specialists, resource centre staff, language specialists, autism specialists, educational psychologists, medical staff, psychotherapists, behavioural managers, emotional support teams, language support, mentors, dyslexia support, transition staff, careers guidance and benefits advisors. Professional vested interest and parental pressures have supported this expansion, as have human and civil rights legislation. Governments until recently have acquiesced in the expense involved in this expansion.

While the majority of lower attainers in all the schools systems studied here were from working- or non-working-class households, the elaborated SEN industry has been driven by middle class and aspirant parents, who now demand assistance and resources for their children who are not likely to achieve required levels of certification, or go on to higher education. The competitive nature of a market-driven school system has created legitimate fears that their children will not be able to move to higher-level courses or find and keep paid work. This is as yet an unremarked effect of increasingly competitive education systems. But despite their fears, middle-class parents, who historically avoided the placement of their 'less able' children on vocational courses, are still likely to avoid vocational courses, especially at the lower levels. Thus vocational education and training continues to be associated with lower-class, lower-status training and work. This is more obvious in the UK and Malta, and to some extent in the USA, less so in Germany and Finland. In England especially, the historic need of the middle classes to avoid relegation of their children to practical and vocational courses has meant that the academic–vocational divide continued to be synonymous with a class divide. Politicians and parents have not yet caught up with the realisation that policies to raise standards of literacy and numeracy have in fact reduced the dichotomy between the academic and the vocational. Vocational courses at all levels now largely incorporate or require literacy, numeracy and IT skills.[2] In addition, largely due to the influence of a worldwide disability rights movement, young people with physical and sensory disabilities, coming as noted from all social classes, now have more opportunities for training, work experience and employment. Neither have English politicians, in their enthusiasm for a knowledge economy, given much thought to the development of a coherent and respected vocational education and training system for young people at all levels.[3] Governments with respected vocational systems make sure that there are close links with the actual and developing economy and take some responsibility for the state of their economies.

Issues and transitions

The issues facing policy makers, practitioners, administrators and others in the countries visited were very similar – summed up simplistically by the question of what to do with lower-attaining young people in a global economy where even low-skill jobs require qualifications. There were differences in national responses. In England central government was still micro-managing the system but without any overall plans for those who did not achieve the GCSE benchmarks, apart from more punitive threats to schools and colleges, pleas to employers to cooperate on apprenticeship schemes and recruitment, and a careers service expected to guide all young people into some kind of job. Reductions in funding for further education colleges and the ending of schemes which actually encouraged lower attainers to persist with their courses – the Education Maintenance Allowance being crucial – were detrimental to the young people and to the colleges. Policy stress was still on individual and skill deficiencies rather than on the amount and kinds of employment available locally. A rhetoric of disadvantage, non-working families and potential criminality of lower attainers persisted and was divorced from discussion of how to create more local and regional employment. Having realised the costs of special education without an understanding of why it had expanded, reforms are now aimed at reducing funding. In the USA there was an acceptance that low-level jobs existed but that in future they were unlikely to be filled by those with no credentials – for example, janitor's jobs now required a qualification. The individualistic work ethic, stronger than in England, and fewer welfare benefits, encouraged schools and colleges to attempt to prepare the learning disabled and lower attainers for at least a two-year college course or a trade or occupational college. There was more emphasis on transition systems guiding students into work experience and vocational courses from 14–15, and as in the UK, working class, racial and ethnic minorities were more likely to be regarded as lower attainers, to drop out of courses or be prepared for low-level jobs. In Germany the long-standing attention given to vocational education and skill training, and the dual system, made it easier for Federal and State governments to understand the problems occurring with a decline in this system and changes in the economy. These left an increasing number of young people 'in transition' who needed low-level courses and progression to other courses or employment if possible. The future of young people leaving special schools with no qualification was increasingly recognised as a problem, although special school teachers were still resistant to notions of inclusion. Although, as in other countries, the low attainers were likely to be from working-class families and minorities, there was more emphasis on the labour market and its deficiencies rather than focusing on the deficiencies of the young people.

Malta was also grappling with the issue of school drop out at 16 and what to do with lower attainers on an island dedicated to a knowledge economy. With the education system supposedly changing to become less selective there was still a stress, as in England, on students achieving in academic subjects, although ironically, just as in England the Secretary of State announced that vocational courses would no longer be equivalent to academic ones, BTEC vocational courses were introduced in Maltese schools. Although not successful in keeping all students in education or training post-16, the Malta College of Arts, Science and Technology was successful in offering a range of vocational courses at all levels, and as elsewhere Malta had an expanded number of professionals dealing with the disengaged and disruptive.

The Finnish education system stood out as ideologically different from the other countries. The egalitarian assumption was that all young people were to be valued, whatever their learning problems, and educated to the highest possible level to age 19, either in upper secondary schools aimed at university, or in vocational colleges with possible progression to higher education. However, although the language of social class was not used, children from working class and immigrant families were more likely to attend the vocational colleges and be prepared for a service economy rather than professional 'knowledge economy' jobs. Although all students who complete vocational courses are qualified for a job, the global recession since 2008 affected all countries, Finland included. Fewer jobs were available, there was less congruence between education, vocational training and the labour market and the government was concerned about increasing youth unemployment. Students who were disaffected or disruptive were regarded as problematic, and formed the majority of drop outs from colleges. A major contrast between Finland and Germany and the other countries was that their teachers were highly qualified, well thought of, and supported by government and parents. In England and the USA, in particular, government regarded teachers in state schools with suspicion and often denigration, and encouraged parents to act as critics and vigilantes rather than as partners in the education of their children.

Discussants in this study were not policy makers, apart from two former Ministers, and were often cynical and critical of the politicians, civil servants and advisers, who were responsible for pushing policy change with no consultation, untested innovations and funding changes onto schools and colleges. They were however, in a position to 'adjust' policy as far as possible, to benefit students. Those in centralised systems (England, Malta) were less happy with the extent of their influence than in decentralised systems (Germany, USA, Finland). The school and college personnel in all the countries took the view that they were dealing with large groups of young people who were often in 'transition to nowhere' in terms of their gaining employment at any but lower levels, or any form of lasting paid employment. Nevertheless, principals, heads, teachers, tutors and administrators were committed to developing courses and work experience that might lead to progression onto the higher-level courses and qualifications employers now required. Although realistic about the likely futures of their students and concerned that policy makers seldom had clear ideas or plans for lower attainers, they did not believe that all low-level work was necessarily exploitation, or 'flexploitation' as Ross (2009) suggested. Low-attaining students in the USA might be in preparation for the five Fs (fast food, cleaning, laundry, messenger and office work) and in common with the other countries, for motor vehicle maintenance, construction, carpentry, bricklaying, painting, hairdressing, social care, sport, gardening, horticulture, pool-cleaning, removal services, janitors, animal welfare assistants, hotel and catering and many other areas, but this was a preparation for work and courses included work experience. It was noteworthy that there was no suggestion that the young people should be prepared for the jobs migrant workers have traditionally taken up – seasonal agricultural work for example.[4] As other studies have found, social and leisure activities were of great importance to young people and holding a low-wage, low-skill job was regarded as a way to finance social activity. While this might be a source of anxiety to policy makers, they could note that the importance of creative industries, regarded as in the forefront of knowledge economies, depended a good deal on leisure activity.[5]

A knowledge economy? Pointless rhetoric for lower attainers?

While this study could not cover the very large literature on developing labour markets in modern economies or the divisions into high-skill and low-skill markets (see for example Ashton 1995, Marsden 2007, Guile 2010, Holmes and Mayhew 2010), there was considerable scepticism of the assumptions by governments that raised educational standards and constant upskilling would automatically improve national competitiveness in a global economy. For those fortunate enough to be part of a knowledge economy, however contentious its definitions, higher levels of education were taken for granted. But for the discussants in this study the constant assertions that all must be prepared for a knowledge economy was pointless rhetoric as far as lower attainers were concerned and indicated a lack of understanding of the relationship between education and the labour market. Discussants took the view that while there had been a massive expansion of human knowledge over the past 150 years, many of those classed as lower attainers had always had a specific place in the production and development of this knowledge. While the aim was to help lower attainers onto college or vocational courses with possibilities of progression, an aim often impeded rather than assisted by government, lower attainers would continue to take the lower skill but necessary jobs. Historically much low-skilled work had underpinned the Industrial Revolution, in the twentieth century there had been a perfection of the internal combustion engine, a global motor industry, an aviation and aircraft industry, military and warfare advances including the H-bomb, space exploration, satellite technology, vaccination, pharmaceutical, biogenetic and medical technologies, food and agricultural technologies and much more. All these required manual and low-skill workers as well as higher levels of knowledge. Nuclear reactors were built with semi-skilled labour; pig-breeding genetics meant larger pigs to be cared for by farm labourers! While Ross (2009) has argued that only a small minority of workers can expect job security and even the higher skilled are part of a 'global precariat', discussants tended to agree with Doogan (2009) that while many economies are blighted by recession, redundancies and bad working practices, there is still some stability and possible employment for lower attainers. Hairdressing in the UK, for example, often used as an example of lower-skilled work, employs some 250,000 mainly young people, and generates £5 billion of sales annually. Important questions may centre around how far young lower attainers had improved their literacy, numeracy, vocational and social skills enough to make them attractive to employers, but it was also important as to how they would be treated in terms of job security, wages and status. In England a familiar rhetoric continued to centre around the need to increase the social mobility of those 'disadvantaged' by their family, housing, and educational circumstances (translated as non-working households on council estates or in inner cities, in less-well resourced schools), with assumptions that the aim for the 'bright' disadvantaged should be an academic education. This assumption has always damaged the reputation of vocational education, and it is unsurprising that public and parental awareness linked vocational qualifications to low-status and possible low-wage jobs. There were however signs that views may be changing, as all parents now worry that their children should obtain jobs. Apprenticeships and vocational courses with work experience and links with employers, have begun to look as attractive as attending a university. This is especially the case for the lower attainers, who are likely to look for work locally. There has been little focus on wages for low-skill jobs, governments and many employers taking the view that low-skill jobs can be remunerated by a low wage, and unions being more concerned to defend wages for the higher skilled. In a democracy the issue should be raised as to why important jobs – keeping cities clean, caring for the old and severely disabled, working in food and agriculture that feeds people – should not be offered a decent basic wage.

Fitting in the lower attainers. Flexicurity revisited?

Economic policy and practice in the UK and USA especially has been driven by a competitiveness agenda and centred on the rhetoric of a knowledge-based economy, which resulted in minimal interest in vocational educational and in particular, in those who would take lower-level courses and do the lower-skilled jobs. There is no shortage of information on the nature of low-skill work, although there are conflicting accounts of numbers in the workforce. In a study of low-wage work in six countries (Gautié and Schmitt 2010), the USA recorded 25 per cent in low-wage employment, although Farrell claimed that 45 per cent of the US workforce were in low wage jobs and 'the split between the haves and have nots in the workplace could not be more dramatic' (Farrell 2010). In Germany 22.7 per cent were recorded as low waged, partly explained by new labour laws allowing part-time low-paid mini jobs. In England around 22 per cent were recorded as in low wage jobs (Lloyd, Marsden, Mayhew 2008), and a study for the Rowntree Trust suggested that those taking these jobs had few or no qualifications and had negative experiences of schooling (Shildrick, MacDonald, Webster, Garthwaite 2010). It is of note, however, that while there has been a focus on raising aspirations attainments of lower attainers, in the current economic situation many young people and their families have an immediate concern to actually find a job.

If lower attainers are to be satisfactorily fitted into national economies, even at the lower end, the relationships between education, training and the labour market become crucial. It is crucial as to how far local, national and regional economies are able to create and absorb labour. Governments have frequently produced arguments that promoting business demand in some regions was pointless if the skills were not available, whereas evidence has indicated that a lack of local jobs and employer participation in training was a major barrier to young people's employment. In Western countries by 2012, economic crises had increased a focus on the whole economy, and debates over austerity measures versus economic growth in all sectors took precedence over discussion of knowledge economies. However the arguments are resolved, consideration will need to be given to those lower-attaining young people who, no matter what progression they make on courses, will continue to function in lower-skilled but necessary jobs. Esping-Anderson reported in 2007 that the labour market position of the low-skilled was deteriorating, and other commentators have deplored their continuing disadvantages (Esping-Anderson 2007). Others are more positive and have more positive ideas as to how capitalist economies can grow for all workers whether employed in private or state enterprises. Flaschel and his colleagues believe that 'free market capitalism need not be accompanied by the social degradation of part of the workforce, through long term unemployment, atypical employment or other forms of alienated work' (Flaschel, Greiner and Luchtenberg 2012: 1). They envisage a flexicurity system where there is no unemployment and workers at all levels have a meaningful occupation and a sufficient income. The concept of flexicurity was introduced by the Danish Prime Minister Paul Rasmussen in the early 1990s and taken up by economists and by the EU Social Policy Commission. This Commission envisaged more partnerships between employers and employees and others, where all partners discussed work organisation at all levels so that there could be growth and profit, with flexible working but security for all employees. Discussions of flexicurity models have stressed the need for a basic wage (not a minimum wage) for all and an end to the 'degradation' forced on the lower-skilled by low wages and insecurity. The Flaschel model assumes a competitive environment with income, employment and security for all in which there are elites of higher skilled and educated people who are aware of their citizenship obligations and act for the benefit of all. Flaschel and his colleagues have no doubt that 'the current situation of worldwide capitalism, in democratic as well as non-democratic societies is characterised by a massive failure in elite behaviour' (ibid: 18). This massive failure was noted in Chapter 1, as the advantages grabbed by global elites, and especially the greed of financial elites, was responsible for much of the degradation of many. The model assumes that the state is the 'employer of first resort' which provides jobs for those not in private industry, unemployed or retired but still wishing to work, and there is a private flexible market still committed to a social structure of accumulation – profit-making – but working long term for the good of the whole society.[6] A flexicurity model continues to attract interest. In the UK Will Hutton, Principal of Hertford College Oxford and a former director of the Work Programme, advocated flexicurity in an article in 2012, as it 'combines greater work place flexibilities with higher unemployment benefits, greater training and job guarantee' (Hutton 2012). Hutton also envisaged a new social contract giving individuals the means to mitigate the risks of unemployment, old age, homelessness and disability. It would include ending current policies that remove much help for those with disabilities and those who will never be able to work. In England in particular, new thinking is needed to move beyond hand-wringing that social mobility has stalled, schools are failing and many young people are demotivated or disruptive ignorant yobs. Attention must be given to developing an economy that can employ all its citizens, including lower attainers, with more respect and less paternalism or insult, and care for those who may not be employable but are still worthy citizens.

Notes

1 A rhetoric of 'broken Britain' dominates government policy concerning work and welfare. Non-working families, welfare dependence, lower-attaining rioting young people and 'the caricature of the slobbish single mother who milks the benefit system' (Jones 2011: 11), currently take precedence over serious analysis of economic and social structures that produce inequalities. An article on the front page of *The Sunday Times* in 2012 announced that 'Public gets new powers to fight yobs', referring to increased powers of individuals to complain if they think that young people are engaging in antisocial behaviour (Leppard 2012).

2 Some observed examples: motor vehicle maintenance courses require an understanding of computer technology, cooking classes for those with moderate learning difficulties require some reading of recipes, servicing lawnmowers requires reading of a handbook, making deckchairs requires some knowledge of measurement and geometry.

3 The government response to the Wolf report (DfE 2011) included a reiteration of the requirement for all young people to obtains GCSEs in English and Maths, and the assertion that making vocational courses equivalent to traditional subjects had led to them being regarded as easy options for the less able, despite evidence that students of all abilities appreciated success in these vocational courses. The response went on to assert that 'vocational education is vital to our economy' (DfE 2011b: 1) but then referred only to high-level technical education and apprenticeships.

4 This study did not examine the effects of migrant labour on low-skill work in any of the countries, although there is a large literature and much disagreement on the effects of migrant labour. Green and colleagues (2009) noted that the UK was one of only three members of the expanded European Union not to impose restrictions on European workers, and up to a million migrant workers entered the UK, especially to work in rural areas, leaving those with low skills vulnerable to local competition from these workers.

5 An interesting example was in the Czech Republic in the City of Ostrava, where 53 creative industries developed around an area of leisure activities, discotheques, clubs and bars (Rumpel, Slach, Koutsky 2010). The lucrative gaming industry depends on leisure activity.

6 Flaschel and Luchtenberg have elaborated their ideas for a new kind of social capitalism, synthesising the work of Marx, Keynes and Schumpeter in a book published in 2012 (Flaschel and Luchtenberg 2012).

Bibliography

ACEVO (2012) *Report of a Commission on Youth Unemployment*. London: Association of Chief Executives of Voluntary Organisations.

Archer, M.S. (1979) *The social origins of education systems*. London: Sage.

Archer, M.S. (1988) *Culture and agency*. Cambridge: Cambridge University Press.

Archer, M.S. (2008) 'Education, subsidiarity and solidarity: past, present and future', in (eds) Archer, M.S. and Donati, P., *Pursuing the common good: how solidarity and subsidiarity can work together*. Vatican City: Pontifical Academy of Social Sciences.

Ashton, D. (1995) 'Understanding changes in youth labour markets: a conceptual framework', *Journal of Education and Work*, 6/3:5–23.

Atkins, L. (2009) *Invisible students: impossible dreams*. Stoke-on-Trent: Trentham Books.

Atkins, L. (2010) 'Opportunity and aspiration or the great deception? The case of 14–19 vocational education', *Power and Education*, 2/3:253–264.

Ayres, L.P. (1909) *Laggards in our schools*. Philadelphia, PA: Fell and Co.

Baird, J., Isaacs, T., Johnson, S., Stobart, G., Yu, G., *et al.* (2011) *Policy effects of PISA*. Oxford: Oxford University Centre for Educational Assessment.

Baker-Dearing Educational Trust (2010) *University technical colleges*. London: Conference on University Technical Colleges, February.

Baldachino, G. (1993) 'Social class in Malta: insights into a home-grown relationship, with special reference to education', *Education (Malta)*, 5/1:2–8.

Ball, S.J. (2009) *Education plc: understanding private sector participation in public sector education*. London and New York: Routledge.

Ball, S.J., Macrae, S. and Maguire, M. (2000) *Choice, pathways and transitions post-16*. London: Falmer.

Bartolo, E. (2010a) 'Meet Minister Dolores Potyomkin in education (partly)', *Malta Today*, 7 March.

Bartolo, E. (2010b) 'Too many drop-outs at MCAST', *Malta Today*, 11 July.

Bartolo, P.A., Ferrante, C., Azzopardi, A., Bason, L., Grech, L. and King, M. (2002) *Creating inclusive schools: guidelines for the implementation of the National Curriculum Policy on inclusive education*. Malta: Ministry of Education.

Bathmaker, A.M. (2005) 'Hanging in or shaping the future; defining the role of vocationally-related learning in a knowledge society', *Journal of Educational Policy*, 20/1:81–100.

Beck, U. (2000) *What is globalisation?* Malden, MA: Polity Press.

Beck, U. (2006) *Power in a global age*. Cambridge: Polity Press.

Beloe Report (1960) *Secondary schools examinations other than GCE*. London: HMSO.

Bendix, R. (1966) *Max Weber: an intellectual portrait*. London: Methuen and Co.

Birrell, J. (2010) 'A whirlwind of hate', *The Guardian*, 19 October.

Blanchett, W.J. (2008) 'Foreword: educational inequities; the intersection of disability, race and class', in (ed) Connor, D. J., *Urban narratives; portraits in progress, life at the intersections of learning disability, race and social class*. New York: Peter Lang, xi–xvii.

Bobbitt, P. (2002) *The shield of Achilles*. London: Allen Lane.

Borg, C. and Mayo, P. (2006) *Learning and social difference: challenges to public education and critical pedagogy*. Boulder, CO: Paradigm Press.

Bosel, J. (2008) *Experimentation in 3rd way apprenticeships in North-Rhine Westphalia*. Paper to the Forum on Social Experimentation in Europe, Grenoble, France.

Brantlinger, E.A. (ed.) (2008) *Who benefits from special education? Remediating (fixing) other people's children*. New York: Routledge.

Brown, G. (2010) Interview on the Andrew Marr Show, BBC 1, 3 January.

Brown, P. (1987) *Schooling ordinary kids*. London: Tavistock.

Brown, P., Lauder, H. and Ashton, D. (2011) *The global auction: the broken promises of education, jobs and incomes*. Oxford: Oxford University Press.

Burt, C. (1937) *The backward child*. London: London University Press.

Cabinet Office (2008) *Getting on; getting ahead: a discussion paper analysing the trends and drivers of social mobility*. London: The Cabinet Office.

California Career Technical Education Model (2006) Sacramento, CA: State Department of Education.

Callahan, D. (2004) *The cheating culture; why more Americans are doing wrong to get ahead*. Orlando, FL: Harcourt Press.

Calleja, C. (2010) 'Teachers accuse education ministry of lack of consultation', *The Times of Malta*, 6 July.

Cassen, R. and Kingdom, G. (2007) *Tackling low educational achievement*. York: Joseph Rowntree Foundation.

Castells, M. (1996) *The rise of the networked society*. Oxford: Blackwell.

Central Bank of Malta (2006) *Malta's economy and the path to the Euro*. Valleta: Central Bank of Malta.

Cerfui, C. and Cooper, P. (2006) 'Social, emotional and behavioural difficulties in Malta: an educational perspective', *Journal of Malta Educational Research*, 41/1:18–36.

Chapman, C., Laird, J. and Ramani, A.K. (2011) *Trends in high school drop out and completion rates in the United States*. Washington, DC: Department for Education.

Chircop, J. (2001) 'Shifting the colonial frontiers: the colonial state, schooling, and the Maltese society', in (ed), R.G. Sultana, *Yesterday's schooling: readings in Maltese educational history*. Malta: Minerva Publications.

Christ, L. (2010) 'Harlem charter school bucks the trend', NYC News Channel on the web, ny1.com, 16 February.

City of Birmingham (1977) *Triennial Report of the Careers Service*. Birmingham: Department of Education.

Communities and Victims Panel (2012) *Report on the riots of August 2011*. London: Office of the Deputy Prime Minister.

Connelly, M. (2011) 'Are the tensions of earlier decades still smouldering?', *The Guardian* (*Society*), 17 August.

Connor, D.J. (2008) *Urban narratives: portraits in progress; life at the intersection of disability, race and social class*. New York: Peter Lang.

Crace, J. (2002) 'What's the point?', *The Guardian* (*Society*), 3 December.

Crowther Report (1959) *15–18* London: HMSO.

Daily Telegraph (2011) 'School lotteries hitting middle classes', 15 March.

Darmanin, M. (2002) 'The opportunism of the "glocal": Malta's education policies', *International Studies in the Sociology of Education*, 12/3:277–302.

Darmanin, M. (2003) 'When students are failed: love as an alternative educational discourse', *International Studies in the Sociology of Education*, 13/2:141–170.

Darmanin, M. (2007) 'Catholic schooling and the changing roles of women: perspectives from Malta', in (eds), Grace, G.R. and O'Keefe, J., *International handbook of catholic education*. Dordrecht: Springer.

Darmanin, M. (2009) 'Empowering women: the contribution of contemporary Catholic schools', *International Studies in Catholic Education*, 1/1:85–101.

Darmanin, M. (2010) 'On a hard rock: trying to be radical in a conservative context', in (ed), Sultana, R.G. *Educators of the Mediterranean: up close and personal*. Rotterdam: Sense Publishers.

Dearing, Sir Ron (1996) *Review of Qualifications for 16–19 year olds*. London: School Curriculum and Assessment Council.

Demie, F. and Lewis, K. (2010) 'White working class achievement: an ethnographic study of barriers to learning in schools', *Educational Studies*, 37/3: 245–264.

DES (1978) *Special educational needs* (The Warnock Report). London: HMSO.

Dewsbury, R. and Allen, E. (2011) 'Double whammy as youth jobless breaks 1 million barrier for the first time and Britain faces one in three chance of a double-dip recession', *Daily Mail*, 16 November.

DfCSF (2009) *Breaking the link between disadvantage and low attainment*. London: Department for Children, Schools and Families.

DfCSF (2010) *Breaking the link between special educational needs and low attainment*. London: Department for Children, Schools and Families.

DfE (2010) The importance of teaching. Cmd 7980, White Paper. London: Department for Education, March.

DfE (2011a) Support and aspiration; a new approach to special educational needs and disability. Cmd 8027. London: Department for Education, May.

DfE (2011b) *The Wolf review of vocational education: the government response*. London: Department for Education.

DfEE (1999) *Learning to succeed: a new framework for post-16 learning*. London: Department for Education and Employment.

DfES (2003) *Opportunity and Excellence 14–19*. London: The Stationery Office.

DfES (2004) *The common assessment framework for children and young people*. London: DfES.

DfES/DTI (2003) *21st century skills: realising our potential*. London: The Stationery Office.

Doogan, K. (2009) *New capitalism; the transformation of work*. Cambridge: The Polity Press.

Dorling, D. (2010) *Injustice: why social inequality persists*. Bristol: The Policy Press.

Doward, J. (2012) 'Criminal past and rich tastes of boss in Jubilee steward row', *The Observer*, 10 June.

DTI (1998) *Our competitive future: building a knowledge-driven economy.* London: Department of Trade and Industry.

Eccleston, K., Hayes, D. (2008) *The dangerous rise of therapeutic education.* London: Routledge.

Economist, The (2009) 'Ready, set go: Barack Obama Chief tries to incite dramatic reform that will last', *The Economist*, 3 October.

Economist, The (2010a) 'From bad to worse', *The Economist*, 3 April.

Economist, The (2010b) 'Leave them kids alone: a set-back for German education reformers', *The Economist*, 24 July.

Egerton Commission (1889) *Report of the Royal Commission on the Blind, Deaf, Dumb and others in the United Kingdom*, 4 vols. London: HMSO.

Elliott, L. (2009) 'Banking on a green industrial revolution', *The Guardian*, 30 November.

Ertl, H. (2000) 'Vocational education and training in Eastern Germany: some reasons and explanations for current problems', in (ed) D. Phillips, *Education in Germany since unification.* Oxford: Symposium Books.

Ertl, H. (2004) 'Tradition and reform: modernising the German dual system of vocational education', in (eds), G. Hayward and S. James, *Balancing the skills equation: key issues and challenges for policy and practice.* Bristol: Policy Press.

Ertl, H. (2009) *After the dual system: notes on aspects of the German skills policy.* Paper to SKOPE Public Policy Forum. Oxford: University of Oxford, Department of Education, 21 October.

Ertl, H. and Phillips, D. (2000) 'The enduring nature of the tripartite system of secondary education in Germany; some explanations', *British Journal of Educational Studies*, 48/4:391–412.

Esping-Anderson G. (2007) 'Rethinking the welfare state', in (eds) Pearce, N. and Margo, J., *Politics for a new generation.* London: Palgrave Macmillan.

Farrell, L. and Fenwick, T. (2007) *Educating the global workforce: knowledge, knowledge work and knowledge workers. World Education Yearbook 2007.* London and New York: Routledge.

Farrell, C. (2010) 'The splits between the haves and have-nots in the workplace couldn't be more dramatic', *The Financial Times (Business Week)*, 1 December.

Fennell, E. (2010) 'Life-long learning is the way forward', *The Times (Focus Report)* 14 July.

Finegold, D., Keep, E. and Miliband, D. (1991) *A British Baccalaureate.* London: IPPR.

Flaschel, P. and Luchtenberg, S. (2012) *Roads to social capitalism: theory, evidence and policy.* Cheltenham: Edward Elgar Publishing.

Flaschel, P. Greiner, A. and Luchtenberg, S. (2012) 'Flexicurity societies, educational formation and the role of elites', *Review of Political Economy*, 24:85–111.

Florida, R.L. (2002) *The rise of the creative class.* New York: Basic Books.

Fuchs, D., Fuchs, L. and Compton, D. (2011) 'Smart RTI: a next-generation approach to multi-level prevention', *Exceptional Children*, 78/3:263–279.

Fuller, A. and Unwin, L. (2009a) 'Change and continuity in apprenticeships: the resilience of a model of learning', *Journal of Education and Work*, 22/5: 405–416.

Fuller, A. and Unwin, L. (2009b) *Creating and supporting expansive apprenticeships: a guide for employers, training providers and colleges*. London: National Apprenticeship Service.

Fuller, B. and Rubinson, R. (1992) *The political construction of education: the state, school expansion and economic change*. New York: Greenwood Press.

Gates, B. (2010) Interview with Bill Gates. BBC TV, Davos, Switzerland, January.

Gautié, J. and Schmitt, J. (2010) *Low wage work in a wealthy world*. New York: Russell Sage Foundation.

Gentleman, A. (2012) 'Charity chief quits over fit-for-work tests', *The Guardian*, 11 April.

Giddens, A. (1994) 'Foreword', in (eds) Sultana, R.G. and Balachino, G., *Maltese Society: a sociological enquiry*. Malta: Minerva Publications.

Ginsberg, F. and Rapp, R. (2009) *Cultural innovation and learning disability*. Learning Disability and New York City Project. New York: Department of Anthropology, New York University.

Gould, S.J. (1981) *The mismeasure of man*. London: Penguin Books.

Graham, J. and Jahnukainen, M. (2011) 'Wherefore art thou, inclusion? Analysing the development of inclusive education in New South Wales, Alberta and Finland', *Journal of Educational Policy*, 26/2:263–228.

Grech, M. (2010) 'A message from the principal; Professor Maurice Grech', in *MCAST Prospectus, 2010–2011*, Malta, p. 13.

Green, A. (1990) *Education and state formation*. New York: St Martins Press.

Green, A. and Steedman, H. (1997) *Into the 21st century. An assessment of British skill profiles and prospects*. London: Centre for Economic Performance, London School of Economics.

Green, A., Preston, J. and Janmaat, J.G. (2006) *Education, equality and social cohesion; a comparative analysis*. London: Palgrave Macmillan.

Green, A., De Hoyes, M., Jones, P. and Owen, R. (2009) 'Rural development and labour supply challenges: the role of non-UK migrants', *Regional Studies*, 43/10:1261–1273.

Guile, D. (2010) *Questioning the simplistic links between qualifications and labour market entry*. London: Centre For Learning and Life Chances in Knowledge Economies and Society, Institute of Education.

Hagermann, K., Jarausch, K.H. and Allemann-Ghionda, C. (2010) *Children, families and states: time policies of childcare, pre-school and primary schooling in Europe*. New York: Berghahn Books.

Ha-Joon Chang (2011) *23 things they don't tell you about capitalism*. Harmondsworth: Penguin Books.

Hall, N.J. and Parker, L. (2007) 'Rethinking No Child Left Behind using critical race theory', in (ed) Sleeter, C., *Facing accountability in education: democracy and equity at risk*. New York: Teachers College Press Columbia University.

Harker, L. (2010) Press release. *New analysis reveals record numbers unable to find work*. London: Institute for Public Policy Research.

Harris, J. (2012) 'Nice work if you can get it', *The Guardian* (*G2*), 22 March.

Hartz, P. (2010) *Committee for Modern Services in the Labour Market*. Bonn: Federal Government Labour Office.

Hautamäki, J., Harjunen, E., Hautamäki, A., Karjalainen, T., Kupiainen, S., *et al.* (2008) *PISA 06. Finland.* Helsinki: Ministry of Education Publications.

Hayward, G., Wilde, S. and Williams, R. (2008) *Engaging youth enquiry.* Oxford: Nuffield/Rathbone.

Herrnstein, R.J. and Murray, C. (1994) *The bell curve. Intelligence and class structure in American life.* New York: The Free Press.

Higham, J., Kremer, H. and Yeomans, D. (2009) *Exploring intermediate vocational education and training for 14–19 year olds in Germany and England.* Paper to European Education Research Conference, Vienna, September.

HM Treasury and Department for Work and Pensions (2003) *Full employment in every region.* London: HMSO.

Holmes, C. and Mayhew, K. (2010) *Are labour markets polarising?* Oxford: SKOPE, Department of Education, University of Oxford.

House of Commons Children Schools and Families Committee (2009–2010) *Young people not in education, employment or training (eighth report).* London: The Stationery Office.

Hudson, R. (2011) 'From knowledge-based economy to . . . knowledge-based economy? Reflections on changes and developments in the economy, and development policies in the north east of England', *Regional Studies*, 45/7:997–1012.

Humphries, S. (1981) *Hooligans or rebels?* Oxford: Blackwell.

Hursh, D. (2005) 'The growth of high-stakes testing in the USA; accountability, markets and the decline of educational equality', *British Educational Research Journal*, 31/5:605–622.

Hurt, J. (1988) *Outside the mainstream: a history of special education.* London: Batsford.

Hutton, W. (2012) 'Osborne is intellectually broken and the real enemy of business', *The Observer*, 29 April.

Idriss, C. (2002) 'Challenges and changes in the German vocational system since 1990', *Oxford Review of Education*, 28/4:473–490.

ILO (2004) *Economic security for a better world.* Geneva: International Labour Office.

ILO (2010) *World youth joblessness soars.* Geneva: International Labour Office.

Individuals with Disabilities Education and Improvement Act (2004) *US. IDEA.* Washington, DC: State Department of Education.

Institute of Fiscal Studies (2010) *The pupil premium; assessing the options.* London: IFS.

IPPR (2009) *Trends in part time and temporary work.* London: Institute for Public Policy Research.

Jahnukainen, M. (2012) 'Special education in Finland', in (eds) Reynolds, C.R., Vannest, K.J., Fletcher-Janzen, E., *Encyclopaedia of Special Education.* Hoboken, NJ: Wiley and Sons.

Jappinen, A.K. (2010) 'Preventing early leaving in VET: distributed pedagogical leadership in characterising five types of successful organisations', *Education and Training*, 62/3:299–312.

Jessop, B. (2002) *The nature of the capitalist state.* Cambridge: Polity Press.

Johnson, E. (1998) *Chicago metropolis 2020. Preparing metropolitan Chicago for the 21st century; executive summary.* Chicago, IL: Commercial Club of Chicago.

Jones, O. (2011) *Chavs: the demonization of the working classes.* London: Verso.

Judt, T. (2005) *Post-war; a history of Europe since 1945.* London: Vintage.

Kamin, L.J. (1974) *The science and politics of IQ.* Harmondsworth: Penguin Books.

Kollowe, J. (2010) 'Germany powers recovery while joblessness holds back America', *The Guardian (Financial)*, 14 August.

Kormann, R. (2003) 'Zur Ueberrepraiesentation auslaendischer kinder und jungendlicher, jugendlicher in Sonderschulen mit demschewerpunkt lernen', in (ed) G. Auernheirmer, *Schieflagen im Bildungssystem: Die Benachteiligung der Migrantkinder.* Opladen: Leske und Budrich.

Kupfer, A. (2010) 'The socio-political significance of changes in the vocational education system in Germany', *British Journal of Sociology of Education*, 31/1:85–97.

Labour Force Survey (2007) London: Office for National Statistics.

Lamb, B. (2009) *Enquiry into special educational needs and parental confidence.* London: Department for Children Schools and Families.

Lazerson, M. (1983) 'The origins of special education', in (eds) Chambers, J.G. and Hartman, W. T. *Special education policies; their history, implementation and finance.* Philadelphia, PA: Temple University Press.

Laukkanen, R. (2008) 'Finnish strategy for high level education for all', in (eds) Soguel, N. and Jaccard, P., *Governance and performance of education systems.* Dordrecht: Springer.

Lawton, D. (2005) *Education and Labour Party ideologies 1900–2001 and beyond.* London: Routledge.

Lawy, R., Quinn, J. and Dement, K. (2009) 'Listening to the "thick bunch": (mis) understanding and (mis) representation of young people in jobs without training in the South West of England', *British Journal of Sociology of Education*, 30/6: 741–755.

Leadbetter, C. (2000) *Living on thin air.* London: Viking.

Leitch, S. (2006) *Prosperity for all: world class skills. Final report.* London: The Stationery Office.

Leonard Cheshire Disability Foundation (2009) *Ready to start project (2006–2009).* London: Leonard Cheshire Disability Company.

Leppard, D. (2012) 'Public gets new powers over yobs', *The Sunday Times*, 20 May.

Linden, C.G. (2011) 'Finnish Presidency to continue fight against youth unemployment', *Nordic Labour Journal (news)*, February.

Lipman, P. (2004) *High stakes education; inequality, globalisation and urban school reform.* London: Routledge Falmer.

Little, A. (2009) 'Spatial patterns of economic activity and inactivity in Britain', *Regional Studies*, 43/7:877–898.

Lloyd, C., Marsden, G. and Mayhew, K. (2008) *Low-wage work in the United Kingdom.* New York: Russell Sage Foundation.

Losen, D.J. and Orfield, G. (2010) *Racial inequality in special education.* Cambridge, MA: Harvard Educational Press (3rd printing).

Luchtenberg, S. (2005) *Migration, citizenship and civic education in multicultural Germany*, Arbeitspapier 5. Essen: Institute fur Migrationsforschung, Interculturelle Padagogik und Zweisprachendidaktik, University of Essen.

Luchtenberg, S. (ed.) (2004) *Migration, education and change.* London: Routledge.

Maguire, S. and Thompson, J. (2006) *Paying young people to stay on in schools. SKOPE Research Paper no. 69.* Oxford: University of Oxford Department of Economics.

Malik, S. (2011) 'Two months without pay: welcome to the new world of work experience', *The Guardian*, 17 November.

Malta 'Smart Innovations' (2011) *Supplement for The Guardian*. On behalf of the Report Company, 23 September.

Mandeville, B. (1714/1988) 'An essay on charity and charity schools', in (ed) Mandeville, B., *The fable of the bees*. Indianapolis, IN: Liberty Classics.

Mannitz, S. (2004) 'Collective solidarity and the construction of social identities in schools: a case study of immigrant youth in post-unification West Berlin', in (ed) S. Luchtenberg, *Migration, education and change*. London: Routledge.

Marginson, S. (1999) 'After globalisation: emerging politics of education', *Journal of Education Policy*, 14/1:19–31.

Marsden, D. (2007) 'Labour segmentation in Britain; the decline of occupational labour markets and the spread of "entry tournaments"', *Economy and Societies*, 28:965–998.

Marx, K. (1887) *Capital: a critical analysis of capitalist production, Vol. 1*. London: Swan, Sonnenschien, Lowry and Co.

McCullough, G. (1998) *Failing the ordinary child; the theory and practice of working class secondary education*. Buckingham: Open University Press.

Mead, L. (1986) *Beyond entitlement: the social obligations of citizenship*. New York: Free Press.

Ministry of Education (1946) *The nation's schools*. London: HMSO.

Ministry of Education, Culture and Sport (2007) *Special schools reform*. Malta: Department of Student Services.

Ministry of Education, Culture and Sport (2009) *Special schools reform*. Malta: Department of Student Services.

Moxley, D. and Finch, J. (eds) (2003) *Sourcebook of rehabilitation and mental health practices*. New York: Plenum Books.

Munoz, V. (2007) *New UN report on German education*. Geneva: United Nations Human Rights Council.

Murray, J. (2011) 'Peter Laeuner: his story', *FE Weekly*, November, available from http://feweek.co.uk/2011/11/11/peter-lauener-his-story/#. Accessed 19 September 2012.

Murray, J. (2012) 'A lick of paint for apprenticeships' image', *The Guardian* (Education), 7 February.

NCPE (National Commission for the Promotion of Equality) (2006) *Family-friendly measures in the workplace*. Malta: NCPE.

Neather, E.J. (2000) 'Change and continuity in education after Wende', in (ed) D. Phillips, *Education in Germany since unification*. Oxford: Symposium Books.

Nokelainen, P. (2011) *Modelling vocational excellence: Finnish perspectives*. Paper to the ESRC/SKOPE conference on Developing Vocational Excellence. London, November.

Oakes, J. (1985) *Keeping track: how schools structure inequality*. New Haven, CT: Yale University Press.

OECD (2005) *Education at a glance*. Paris: OECD.

Ofsted (2010) *Special educational needs and disability review*. London: Office for Standards in Education.

Oliver, M. (1990) *The politics of disablement*. London: Macmillan.

Oliver, M. and Barnes, C. (2010) 'Disability studies, disabled people and the struggles for inclusion', *British Journal of Sociology of Education*, 31/5:547–560.

Parzych, H. (1997) *Who are you calling LD?* San Antonio, TX: PLC Educational Publishing.

Pfahl, L. and Powell, J.W. (2011) 'Legitimating school segregation: the special education profession and the discourse of learning disability in Germany', *Disability and Society*, 26/4:449–462.

Powell, J.W. (2010) 'Changes in disability classification. Redrawing categorical boundaries in special education in the United States and Germany', *Comparative Sociology*, 9:241–267.

Powell, J.W. (2011) *Barriers to inclusion.* Boulder, CO: Paradigm Publishers.

Pring, R., Hayward, G., Hodgson, A., Johnson, J., Keep, E., *et al.* (2009) *Education for all: the future of education and training for 14–19 year olds.* London: Routledge.

Public Accounts Committee (2009) *Supporting people with autism through adulthood, fifth Report of Session 2008–2009.* London: The Stationery Office.

Pykett, E. (2008) 'Working classes are less intelligent, says evolution expert', *The Scotsman*, 22 May.

Quinn, B. and Malik, S. (2012) 'Parents to control budgets for special educational needs', *The Guardian*, 15 May.

Ramesh, R. (2011) 'Around England: Nottingham', *The Guardian*, 17 August.

Ramesh, R. (2012) 'Community, not ghetto: Remploy workers reject claims of segregation', *The Guardian*, 12 April.

Ravitch, D. (2011) 'What can we learn from Finland?', http:/blogs.edweek/Bridging Differences/2011/10. Accessed 11 October 2012.

RCCCFM (1908) *Report of the Royal Commission on the Care and Control of the Feeble-minded*, 8 vols. London: HMSO.

Reich, R. (1991) *The wealth of nations.* New York: Simon and Schuster.

Rex, J. (1979) 'Sociology, theory, typologies, value standpoints and research', Appendix 1, in Rex, J. and Tomlinson, S., *Colonial immigrants in a British city: a class analysis.* London: Routledge.

Richardson, J.G. and Powell, J.W. (2011) *Comparing special education; from origins to contemporary paradoxes.* Stanford, CA: Stanford University Press.

Rizvi, F. (2007) 'Post colonialism and globalisation in education', *Cultural Studies, Critical Methodologies*, 7/3:256–263.

Robinson, P. (1997) *The myth of parity of esteem. Earnings and qualifications.* Discussion paper no 34. London: Centre for Economic Performance, London School of Economics.

Rogers, C. (2011) 'Mothering and intellectual disability; partnership rhetoric', *British Journal of Sociology of Education*, 32/4:563–581.

Rose, S. (2005) *The 21st-century brain.* London: Vintage Books.

Ross, A. (2009) *Nice work if you can get it.* New York: New York University Press.

Rothkopf, D. (2008) *Superclass: the global power elite and the world they are making.* London: Little, Brown.

Rumpel, P., Slach, O. and Koutsky, J. (2010) 'Researching creative industries in the Czech Republic; a case study from the city of Ostrava', *Regions*, 277, Spring: 18–19.

Sabel, C., Saxenian, A., Miettinen, R., Kristensen, P.H. and Hautamäki, J. (2010) *Individualized service provision in the new welfare state: lessons from special education in Finland.* Helsinki: a report prepared for SITRA.

Sacco, J. (2010) 'The unwanted: African migrants trying to reach Europe (cartoon series)', *The Guardian (Weekend)*, 17 July 2010.

Sadler, Sir M. (1916) 'Need we imitate the German system', *The Times*, 14 January.

Sahlberg, P. (2001) 'Education policies for raising student learning: the Finnish approach', *Journal of Education Policy*, 22/2:141–171.

Sarason, S.B. and Doris, J. (1979) *Educational handicap. Public policy and social history.* New York: Free Press.

Schrag, P. and Divoky, D. (1975) *The myth of the hyperactive child and other means of child control.* Harmondsworth: Penguin Books.

Sennett, R. (2006) *The culture of the new capitalism.* New Haven, CT: Yale University Press.

Shepherd, J. (2010) 'Critical friend', *Education Guardian*, 12 January.

Shepherd, J. (2011) 'Finishing school', *Education Guardian*, 22 November.

Shildrick, T., MacDonald, R., Webster, C. and Garthwaite, K. (2010) *The low-pay, no-pay cycle: understanding recurrent poverty.* York: Joseph Rowntree Trust.

Sigmon, S.B. (1990) 'Foundations of education and the mildly learning disabled', in (ed) Sigmon, S.B., *Critical voices on special education.* New York: State University of New York Press.

Simola, H. (2005) 'The Finnish miracle of PISA', *Comparative Education*, 41: 455–470.

Simon, B. (1960) *Studies in the history of education 1780–1870.* London: Lawrence and Wishart.

Simon, B. (1991) *Education and the Social order 1940–1990.* London: Lawrence and Wishart.

Six Degrees (2011) 'The end of Finland as we know it?', *Society (Helsinki)*, June: 10–12.

Sklair, L. (2001) *The transnational capitalist class.* Oxford: Blackwell.

Slee, R. (2011) *The irregular school.* London: Routledge.

Sleeter, C.E. (1986) 'Learning disabilities; the social construction of a special education category', *Exceptional Children*, 53:46–54.

Sleeter, C.E. (1987) 'Why is there learning disability; a critical history of the birth of the field', in (ed) T.S. Popkewitz, *The formation of the school subject matter; the struggle for an American institution.* Balcombe: Falmer Press.

Spencer, F.H. (1938) *An Inspectors testament.* London: Longman.

Standing Conference of Ministers of Education and Culture (2009) *Review of special education.* Bonn: Ministry of Education and Culture.

Standing Conference of the Ministry of Education and Cultural Affairs of the Lander in the Federal Republic of Germany (2009) *Basic structure of the education system in the Federal Republic of Germany.* Bonn: Standing Conference of the Ministry of Education and Cultural Affairs of the Lander in the Federal Republic of Germany.

Statistisches Bundesamt Deutschland (2007) *Bildung und Kultur.* Weisbaden: Germany.

Steinberg, S. (2010) 'Higher learning without college', *New York Times*, 23 May.

Stiglitz, J.E. (2002) *Globalisation and its discontents.* Harmondsworth: Penguin Books.

Stiglitz, J.E. (2007) *Making globalisation work.* New York: Norton Press.

Studio Schools Trust (2010) *The Studio Schools model.* London: The Studio Schools Trust.

Sultana, R.G. (1998) 'Education and social cohesion in a micro-state', *Education and Society*, 16/1:3–14.

Sultana, R.G. (2001) 'Technical and vocational education in nineteenth-century Malta', in (ed) Sultana, R.G., *Yesterday's schools: readings in Maltese educational history*. Malta: PEG Ltd.

Sultana, R.G. (ed) (2010) *Educators of the Mediterranean: up close and personal*. Rotterdam: Sense Publications.

Sultana, R.G. and Baldachino, G. (eds) (1994) 'Introduction', in *Maltese Society: a sociological enquiry*. Malta: Minerva Publications.

Summerfield, P. and Evans, E. (eds) (1990) *Technical Education and the State since 1850*. Manchester: Manchester University Press.

Taylor, M.E. (1981) *Education and work in the Federal Republic of Germany*. London: St Stephen's House Press.

Times of Malta (2009) 'No student left behind', 28 October.

Tomlinson, M. (2004) *Curriculum and qualifications reform. Final report of the working group on 14–19 reform*. Nottingham: DfES.

Tomlinson, S. (1985) 'The expansion of special education', *Oxford Review of Education*, 11/2:157–166.

Tomlinson, S. (1996) 'Conflicts and dilemmas for professionals in special education', in (eds) Christensen, C and Rizvi, F., *Disability and the dilemmas of social justice* Buckingham: Open University Press.

Tomlinson, S. (2005) *Education in a post-welfare society*, 2nd edn. Maidenhead. Open University Press/McGraw-Hill.

Tomlinson, S. (2008) *Race and education: policy and politics in Britain*. Maidenhead: Open University Press/McGraw-Hill

Tomlinson, S. (2010a) *NEETS, yobs and cripples; low attainers in a global knowledge economy*. London: The Leverhulme Trust.

Tomlinson, S. (2010b) 'Die global wirtschaft, minderheiten und bildung', in (eds) Amos, S.K., Meseth, W., Proske, M., *Oeffentliche Erziehung revisited*. Wiesbaden: V.S.Verlag.

Tomlinson, S. (2012a) 'The irresistible rise of the SEN industry', *Oxford Review of Education*, 38/4:1–20.

Tomlinson, S. (2012b) *A sociology of special education*. London: Routledge.

Tomlinson, S. (ed.) (1997) *Education 14–19: critical perspectives*. London: The Athlone Press.

Topping, A. (2011) 'Middle class happy with rampant inequality', *The Guardian*, 16 March.

Traynor, I. (2012) 'Say fromage: meet the EU's extended family', *The Guardian G2*, 1 February.

Tredgold, A.F. (1908) *Mental deficiency*, 1st edn. London: Ballière, Tindall and Cox.

Trollope, A. (1858) *The Three Clerks*, Chapter 11, (3 vols). London: Richard Bentley.

Varenne, H. and McDermott, R. (1999) *Successful failure: the schools America builds*. Los Angeles, CA: Westview Press.

Vlaeminke, M. (1990) 'The subordination of technical education in secondary schooling 1870–1939', in (eds) Summerfield , P. and Evans, E.J., *Technical Education and the State since 1850*. Manchester: Manchester University Press.

Walker, P. (2012) 'Anti-disabled abuse fuelled by benefit cuts', *The Guardian*, 6 February.

Weiss, L. (1990) *Working class without work*. New York: Routledge.

Wilkinson, R. and Pickett, K. (2009) *The spirit level: why some societies are more equal than others*. London: Allen Lane.

Willis, P. (1977) *Learning to labour: how working class kids get working class jobs*. Aldershot: Gower Press.

Witte, J. and Kallenberg, A. (1995) 'Matching training and jobs: the fit between vocational education and employment in the German labour market', *European Sociological Review*, 11/3:1–25.

Wolf, A. (2011) *Review of vocational education: The Wolf Report*. London: DfE.

Wolf, A. (2002) *Does Education Matter?* Harmondsworth: Penguin Books.

World Bank (2003) *Life-long learning in the global knowledge economy: challenges for developing countries. A World Bank Report*. Washington: World Bank.

Young, M. (1958) *The rise of the meritocracy*. Harmondsworth: Penguin.

Index